Frederick A. Paley

The Gospel of St. John

a verbatim translation from the Vatican ms., with the notable variations of the

Sinaitic and Beza ms., and brief explanatory comments

Frederick A. Paley

The Gospel of St. John
a verbatim translation from the Vatican ms., with the notable variations of the Sinaitic and Beza ms., and brief explanatory comments

ISBN/EAN: 9783337285241

Printed in Europe, USA, Canada, Australia, Japan

Cover: Foto ©Lupo / pixelio.de

More available books at **www.hansebooks.com**

THE GOSPEL OF ST. JOHN.

THE GOSPEL OF ST. JOHN;

A VERBATIM TRANSLATION FROM THE VATICAN MS.

With the Notable Variations of the Sinaitic and Beza MS., and Brief Explanatory Comments.

BY

F. A. PALEY, M.A., LL.D.,

EDITOR OF "THE GREEK TRAGIC POETS," ETC., ETC.

LONDON:
SWAN SONNENSCHEIN, LOWREY & CO.,
PATERNOSTER SQUARE.
1887.

Printed by Hazell, Watson, & Viney, Ld., London and Aylesbury.

PREFACE.

THIS work is an entirely new and literal translation of the Fourth Gospel from the text of the Vatican MS. *alone*, which is believed to have been written not later than the age of Eusebius, *i.e.*, early in the fourth century.*

All the noteworthy variations (which in this Gospel are not very numerous) in the famous "Sinaitic" and the equally celebrated "Beza" MSS., the former probably contemporary, the latter of a date perhaps somewhat later, yet

---

* "Nec quicquam inventum iri puto quod obstet, quin Vaticanum codicem pariter atque Sinaiticum circa Eusebii ætatem scriptum esse arbitremur."—Tischendorf, Prolegomena, p. xxxi., ed. Lips., 1867, 4to.

closely representing the text of the second or third century,* have been added in the brief commentary; smaller discrepancies, interesting only to the verbal critic, being purposely omitted.

It is true that the text of this "supremely excellent" Vatican MS. has been generally followed in the Revised Version. But other readings are there admitted, and the brief references given at the foot of each page,—"many ancient authorities read" so-and-so,—leave it open as to what MSS. are meant. The Revised Version, like the Authorised, is "eclectic," and not compiled from one uniform primitive source, as this claims to be. Perhaps, therefore, a new and strictly independent version of this Vatican text may be found to be not without interest. The few and brief comments added are suggestions for thought, not written in the spirit of cavil. A Greek scholar, dealing with this as he would with

---

* Scrivener, Introduction, p. lxiv., ed. 1864, Cambridge

any other ancient document, especially if he is uninfluenced by any motive except the pursuit of truth, has more freedom than the trained theologian, who naturally treats with reserve what he is in a manner bound to regard as an infallible record. From the orthodox point of view Canon Westcott's well-known edition of this Gospel, with its ample commentary, will satisfy every theological student. It was not his object to raise difficulties in the narrative, or to call in question any statement, or to point out the parallels, often extremely striking, in heathen mythology, or to say a word about sun-worship or fish-worship, and the portents connected with them. This is forbidden ground. No one expects to hear from the pulpit, no one ever reads in a theological treatise, of extending the science of comparative mythology so as to include the kindred beliefs of the traditional theology. For myself, I have long been very much struck with, and I have learned heartily to despise, that *suppressio veri* which is but too characteristic of professed orthodoxy. The assumption that the record before you is in some special way exempted from error or mistake in language and fact, is evidently fatal to any fair dealing with the narrative, or to any reasonable criticism of alleged wonders and portents. Every ancient history must speak for itself, and must be received and interpreted according to the knowledge of any given age. In the few notes and explanations I have offered in connexion with ancient and widely-spread superstitions, I have attended only to context and the mind and style of the writer, regarding "doctrine," properly so called, as the province of others. I do not think anything I have said need ause offence to any fair and honest mind.

A large part of Dr. Westcott's work is taken up with corrections of the Authorised Version, which he gives as his text. It has long been acknowledged that, as a translation, this version is not trustworthy, nor is the "textus receptus" (R. Stephen's, 1550) of the Greek of any high value, seeing that in about a thousand passages of this Gospel alone it is at variance with the three ancient copies which, according to Dr. Westcott, are the sole authorities for the text of the second and third centuries.* Those who are so timid about "new views" are bound to remember that for nearly three centuries the clergy have been teaching, and the public have been learning, from a translation replete with mistakes, false readings, and incorrect renderings. Many, in their unreasoning "bibliolatry," have worshipped an idol: it is time to be wiser.

A good translation should not be behind the thought, or idiom, or comparative usages of the time in which it is made. It is in this respect that I have felt the greatest difficulty; and, though I have been unsparing of pains and trouble, I am conscious that many renderings are far from satisfactory. It is impossible

---

* This excludes the Alexandrine MS. of perhaps equal antiquity, but believed to embody a recension which was the source and origin of the readings of the later MSS. generally.

always to observe the mean between the literal sense of a word, and the force evidently intended to be conveyed by it. Very often the English idiom has no exact equivalent, the customs referred to are not our customs,* the tone of thought is wholly different, even the Greek more "crabbed" in style and irregular in syntax than the ordinary classical models. "All endeavours to translate into another tongue must fall short of their aim, when the obligation is imposed of producing a version that shall be alike literal and idiomatic, faithful to each thought of the original, and yet, in the expression of it, harmonious and free."†

The "Revised Version," as its name implies, is not a *new* translation; it is an old and not

---

* For example, the word μύρον, rendered "ointment" in xii. 3, I have translated, less literally but nearer to the meaning, "fragrant essence." The rhetorical antithesis of "hating life" (xii. 25) seems, to an English reader, immoral, and an incentive to suicide, whereas the contrast meant must be that of being too fond of life, and of being indifferent to its pleasures. So perhaps xv. 23 really means, "he that is *indifferent to* me," etc. This *must* be the sense in Luke xiv. 26.

† Preface to "Revised Version."

very accurate one corrected. But it retains, as far as was possible, and from the best motives, the quaintness of a past generation, and not a few renderings which, if they cannot be called wrong, might assuredly have been better. Hence it seems desirable to present the very text of the Greek that we can prove to have been accepted as genuine in the third century, in an English version as close as is consistent with differences of idiom, as clear as the observance of context, emphasis, order of words, and logical connexion can make it, without undue licence, and as plain and simple and modern in style as the subject-matter, sometimes very obscure, will allow.

The English reader must be apprised that some difference in the rendering (occasionally even of the same word) does not, in comparison with the received version, necessarily imply a corresponding difference in the Vatican text, which has been closely and faithfully followed throughout.

Those words (chiefly the pronouns) which

seem to have *emphasis* are printed in italics; those which, to meet the difference of our idiom, are *inserted*, and not in the Greek, are inclosed in brackets, *e.g.* "(Good) woman" for "woman." Very many passages are obscure, or convey a false impression to English readers,* where a too rigid rule is observed in invariably giving the closest rendering of a Greek word by an English word. This is the principle on which the Latin versions were constructed,—a mere mechanical word-change.

No special pains have been taken to give the same English always for a particular word. On the contrary, occasional variations have been made in consideration of context. But "Master" is everywhere substituted for "Lord."

The present translation, as well as the notes, are offered for free criticism, as at least the thoughtful production of one whose whole life has been devoted to the study of Greek.

---

* In xv. 3, καθαροὶ is not "clean," but "clear," as a trimmed vine. "He purgeth it" (A.V.), taken from the Vulgate, is still worse.

I.

1 IN the beginning was the Logos,* and the Logos was in relation to God, and the Logos was God.†

2. It was *he* who at the first‡ stood in relation to God.

---

* Literally, "at first (or, at the beginning of all things) the Logos was in existence." This term, which is quite untranslatable, was introduced, apparently from the Persian theology, by the Alexandrine school of Philo and the neo-Platonists, to express the creative and intelligent action of the Divine Being before the creation of the worlds; or, in other words, God manifested in his works: the writer now identifies the Logos with the manifestation of God in the Christ, or Messiah. The usual translation, "the Word was with God" (from the Latin Vulgate), conveys no clearly intelligible idea. That the Logos was regarded in some mysterious way as a *person* rather than a *principle* (mind or reason), is agreed by the learned.

† That is, perhaps, "not only (as some maintain) stood in relation to God, but actually *was* God." If, therefore, the Christ is the Logos, this gives his claim to be Divine.

‡ Contrasted with the *later* manifestation in Christ. See on viii. 24.

3. All things were made through him, and without him was made not a single thing that has been made.

4. In him was life,* and the life was the light,

5. And the light illuminates in the dark, and the darkness overtook it not.†

6. There came into the world‡ a man sent forth from God ; (and) his name (was) John.

7. *This* (messenger) came for witness,§ that he might bear witness about the light, that all might believe through him.

---

* The Sinaitic and Beza give, "in him is life, and the life was the light of men." A reading of great authority in this difficult passage was to place the stop after "not a single thing," and commence a new sentence, "That which has been made was (or is) life in him." But again, this is hardly, if at all, intelligible.

† In a country and neighbourhood in which sun worship was the ancient religion, not a few terms and even ideas may well be supposed to have passed into Christianity from the solar cult (see on ver. 51). Here, as in 1 John ii., light and darkness are represented as in conflict. For the old-world belief was, that the dragon of darkness pursued the sun to devour it. The common version, "The darkness comprehended (apprehended, R.V.) it not," appears to have been received from the Vulgate.

‡ Literally, "there was born."

§ This special and primary object of his coming is explained in the next clause, and in ver. 8.

8. *He* was not the light, but (was sent) that he might bear witness about that light.

9. That was the real light which lights every man coming into the world.

10. He was in the world, and the world was made through him, and (yet) the world knew him not.*

11. He came into (created) things that were his own, and those who were his own received him not.†

12. But as many as did receive him, to them he gave the privilege to become children of God, (even) to those who believe in his name.

13. Who were begotten not of human parents nor of the will ‡ of the flesh, but from God.

14. And the Logos became flesh and made his abode § among us,—and we beheld his

---

* That is, the world did not know the *real* light (the Logos) was the Christ.

† Literally, "took him not from (the sender)."

‡ *Wish* or *desire* seems to be meant. The Sinaitic and Beza read, "not of blood (bloods), nor of the will of the flesh, nor of the will of a man."

§ Literally, "his tent," or temporary dwelling.

glory, a glory as of an only-begotten* from the Father,—full of (the) grace of truth,†

15. (John bears witness about him, and cries aloud saying, This was he who said,‡ He that comes after me is now before me,§ because he was first in regard to me,)

16. Inasmuch as out of his fulness we all received, and grace for grace,

17. Because the law was given through Moses; (but) that grace and that truth came through Jesus Christ.

18. God (himself) no one has ever yet seen; the only-begotten God, who is in the

---

* Modern research has proved that this term was familiar in the ancient solar cult and vocabulary. One meaning is, "only son;" another is, "born of one parent only," *i.e.*, not by the usual relation of both sexes. This may explain the addition, "from a father."

† The MSS. Sin. and Bez. give "grace and truth," and in the latter "full" agrees with "glory," not with Logos.

‡ The Beza has, "This is he of whom I say," etc.; the Sinaitic, "This was he who comes behind me, who has become before me," etc. This verse (15) must be taken as a parenthesis.

§ Literally, "has become before (in front of) me because he had pre-existence of me." The words seem to refer to the sun and his forerunner, and their change of position.

bosom of the Father, he it is that declared him.*

19. And this is the witness of John, when the Jews sent to him from Jerusalem priests and Levites to ask him, Who art thou?

20. And he confessed and denied not, and confessed,† *I* am not the Christ.

21. And they asked him, What then (art) thou? Art thou Elias? And he said, No. Art thou the prophet? ‡ And he answered, No.

22. They said therefore to him, Who art thou? that we may give a reply to those who sent us. What dost thou say of thyself?

23. Said he, I am the voice of one crying aloud in the wilderness, Make straight the way of the Lord, as said Esaias the prophet.

---

* Literally, "explained him" The Sinaitic as well as the Vat. has "the only-begotten God" (the Beza is wanting here), but there can be little doubt it is an error of transcription. Dr. Westcott's version is arbitrary, "one who is God only-begotten." The true reading must either be, "the only-begotten Son" (the abbreviations of the words being closely alike, υσ and θσ), or, "the only-begotten," without further addition.

† Apparently either this verb or the first clause of the verse is an interpolation. Perhaps, καὶ οὐκ ἠρνήσατο, ἀλλ' ὡμολόγησεν.

‡ Viz., Esaiah, who is so called in 23.

24. And there had been sent forth (some) from the Pharisees,*

25. And they questioned him and said to him, Then why do you baptise, if you are not the Christ nor Elias nor the prophet?

26. John answered them and said, I baptise in water; in the midst of you stands (one) whom you know not,

27. Who is coming after me, of whom *I* am not worthy to untie the thong of his shoe.†

28. These things took place in Bethany on the other side of the Jordan, where John was, baptising.

29. On the morrow he sees Jesus coming to him, and says, See (here is) the Lamb of God who takes away‡ the sin of the world.

30. This is he about whom I said, Behind me is coming a man who has been before

---

* Or, "and they had been sent from among the Pharisees."

† Literally, perhaps, "to whom *I* am not equal (in value or merit) that I should untie." *i.e.*, "or even a fit person to untie," and thus perform a menial office for. For ἄξιος Mark i. 7 has ἱκανός.

‡ Or, "takes (on himself) and bears," etc. An allusion to the Paschal Lamb.

me, in that he was in being first in regard to me.*

31. And I knew him not, but that he might be manifested to Israel, for this I came, baptising in water.

32. And John bare witness, saying, I have myself seen † the Spirit coming down as a dove out of the sky, and it remained on him,

33. And I knew him not; but he who sent me to baptise in water, he said to me, Upon whomsoever you shall have seen the Spirit coming down, and remaining on him, he it is who baptises in the Holy Spirit.

34. And I *have* seen (it), and have borne witness that this is the Son of God.

35. On the morrow again stood John and two of his disciples,

36. And having fixed his eyes on Jesus walking he says, See, (here is) the Lamb of God.

37. And the two disciples heard him speaking, and went along with Jesus.

38. But Jesus having turned and beheld them

---

* Viz., as the Logos.
† "I have beheld" (R.V.).

coming with him, says to them, What seek ye? And they said to him, Rabbi, which means, being interpreted, Teacher, where art thou staying?

39. He says to them, Come, and you shall see. They came therefore and saw where he was staying, and they remained with him for that day: (the time) was about the tenth hour.

40. It was Andrew, the brother of Simon Peter, (who was) one of the two who heard from John, and went with him.

41. This (disciple) finds first his own brother Simon, and says to him, We have found the Messiah, which is, being interpreted, Anointed.

42. (And) he led him to Jesus, (and) Jesus having fixed his eyes on him said, Thou art Simon the son of John; thou shalt be called Cephas, which is explained *Stone*.

43. On the morrow he was minded to go out into Galilee, and he finds Philip,* and Jesus says to him, Come with me.

---

* Perhaps the writer meant, "already there."

44. Now Philip was from Bethsaida, from* the city of Andrew and Peter.

45. Philip (then) finds Nathanael, and says to him, Him of whom Moses wrote in the Law, and the Prophets, we have found,—Jesus son of Joseph, him of Nazareth.

46. And Nathanael said to him, Out of Nazareth can there be anything good? Philip says to him, Come and see.

47. (Now) Jesus had seen Nathanael coming to him, and he says concerning him, See, (here is) truly an Israelite in whom there is no guile.

48. Says Nathanael to him, Whence have you knowledge of me? Jesus answered and said to him, Before Philip called you, when you were under the fig-tree, I saw you.†

49. Nathanael answered him, Rabbi, thou art the Son of God, thou art King of Israel. ‡

---

* Lit., "out of."

† These words seem capable of signifying " even before you were born." There is, perhaps, the same symbolism in the "fig-leaf" of Gen. iii. 7, viz., the ripe fruit concealed under the leaf.

‡ Both terms mean, "Thou art indeed the promised Messiah."

50. Jesus answered and said to him, For that I said to you that I saw you underneath* the fig-tree, do you believe? You shall see greater things than these.

51. And he says to him, Verily, verily, I say to you, ye shall see the heaven opened and the angels of God going up and coming down upon the Son of man.†

---

* Lit., "concealed beneath."

† This extraordinary prophecy seems to have in regard Jacob's vision in Gen. xxviii. 12. One can hardly doubt that in its origin this form of speech was *solar*. Compare iii. 13, 14; Rom. x. 6, 7; Eph. iv. 8-10. The current belief that Elias (Elijah) would return bodily to earth is probably due to the resemblance of the name to Ἥλιος, and the two have the closest associations in the modern Greek Church. This observation applies to the narrative of the Transfiguration, which is strongly tinted with solar imagery (Luke ix. 29, etc.).

II.

1. AND on the third day a marriage took place in Cana of Galilee; and the mother of Jesus was there.

2. And Jesus also was invited and his disciples to the marriage (feast).

3. And when the wine had failed,* the mother of Jesus says to him, They have no wine.

4. And Jesus says to her, What (is that) to me and to thee, (good) woman? † My hour has not yet come.

5. His mother says to the servers, Whatever he may say to you, do.

---

* After "had failed" the Sinaitic adds six words, the reading of which is corrupt and unintelligible. They are marked in the MS. by inverted commas, as an addition.

† The common rendering, "Woman, what have I to do with thee?" and the inferences drawn from it by some, are extremely doubtful. In our idiom, such an answer sounds rude, churlish, and repulsive. Compare iv. 21.

6. Now there were there six stone water jugs, placed there according to the Jews' custom of purifying,* holding two or three firkins apiece.

7. Jesus says to them, Fill up the jugs with water. And they filled them to the top.

8. Again † he says to them, Draw out now, and bring it to the president of the banquet. And they brought it.

9. Now when the president had tasted the water that had become wine, and knew not whence it was, albeit the servers knew, who had drawn the water; he, the president of the banquet, calls the bridegroom

10. And says to him, Every man‡ sets on the good wine first, and when (the guests) have drunk freely,§ the weaker (sort): *you* have kept the *good* wine till now.‖

11. This beginning of his signs did Jesus in

---

* Probably for washing or dipping the hands before the meal.

† "And he saith unto them" (R.V.), which is more literal.

‡ In our idiom, "men generally."

§ Literally, "have become tipsy."

‖ The quantity of wine (and *good* wine) made, between sixty and seventy gallons, *after* the wine at first provided had all been consumed, is a difficulty that may be left to "total

Cana of Galilee, and manifested his glory,* and his disciples believed on him.

12. After this he went down to Capharnaum, himself and his mother and his disciples; and there they stayed for not many days.

13. And the Passover of the Jews was near, and Jesus went up to Jerusalem,

14.† And found in the temple those who were selling oxen and sheep and doves, and the money-changers sitting (at their tables).

15.† And having made a scourge of cords he cast them all out of the temple, both the sheep and the oxen,‡ and poured out the small coins of the money-changers, and overturned their tables,

16. And to those who were selling the doves

---

abstainers" to explain. Dr. Westcott thinks "draw out now" may mean "from the well," and not from the jugs, and that the water was changed into wine "by its destination for use at the feast."

* This obscure phrase seems to mean, " made it plain that he would gain the credit and the reputation of being the Messiah." See on ii. 23.

† A slight variant in the Sinaitic indicates a more ancient reading, " And having found . . . he made," etc.

‡ The Sinaitic reads, " He cast out of the Temple the sheep and the oxen."

he said, Take these things hence; make not the house of my Father a house of merchandise.

17. (Then) remembered his disciples that it is written, The zeal of thy house will devour me.*

18. The Jews therefore answered and said to him, What sign dost thou show us, in that thou doest these things?†

19. Jesus answered and said to them, Demolish this temple and in three days I will raise it up.

20. The Jews therefore said, In forty-six years was this temple built, and wilt thou in three days raise it up?

21. But *he* was speaking about the temple of his body.

22. When therefore he had been raised from the dead, his disciples remembered that he had been saying this, and they had faith in the

---

* Psalm lxix. 9. Perhaps καταφάγεται is future, after the analogy of ἔδομαι.

† "What sign shewest thou unto us, seeing that thou doest these things" (Auth. and Rev. Vers.). This is hardly intelligible. We should expect, "that thou doest these things *from God*," and εκ θυ (ἐκ Θεοῦ) may have dropped out. Compare v. 36.

scripture and in the word which Jesus had spoken.

23. And when he was in Jerusalem at the Passover, the (Jewish) feast, many believed in his name, beholding there* the signs which he was doing.

24. But Jesus himself was not for entrusting himself to them, through his own knowledge of them all,

25. And because he needed not that any one should give testimony about the man [for he himself knew what was in the man.†]

---

* The Greek may also mean, "seeing his signs."

† An exceedingly obscure passage, on which much has been said and written. Perhaps it is corrupt, or interpolated, or both. The words equally well mean, "through all knowing him," which would mean, that his career had become notorious even in Jerusalem, and he might have been arrested. That "the man" means "man" in the general or abstract sense, is very difficult to believe. The last clause, which is supposed to express the prescience of Christ, may perhaps have been added, and the original *may* have been καὶ οὐ χρείαν εἶχον ἵνα τις μαρτυρήσῃ περὶ αὐτοῦ, "because all knew him, and they needed no one to give testimony about him."

III.

1. NOW there was a man of the Pharisees,—Nicodemus (was) his name,—a ruler of the Jews.

2. This man came to him by night and said to him, Rabbi, we know that thou hast come from God (as) a teacher; for* no one can do these signs which thou doest unless God is with him.

3. Jesus answered and said to him, Verily, verily I say unto you, unless one shall have been born anew,† he cannot see the kingdom of God.

---

* The Sinaitic reads, "and (that) no one," etc.

† Or, "from above." The context, *i.e.*, the explanation of Christ in vers. 7, 8, and the use of the word in ver. 31, seem to indicate this latter meaning, while it is clear that Nicodemus took it in the former. The stupidity or unspiritual mind of the Pharisee is perhaps shown by his question. The notion of *life* (ψυχή) being *breath* (πνεῦμα) was a widely

4. Says Nicodemus to him, how can a man be *born* when he is old? Can he enter into his mother's womb a second time and be born?

5. Jesus answered, Verily, verily I say unto you, Unless one be born of water and spirit he cannot enter into* the kingdom of God.

6. That which has been born from the flesh is flesh, and that which has been born from the Spirit is spirit.

7. Marvel not that I said to you, Ye have to be born anew.

8. The wind† blows where it chooses, and you hear its voice, but you know not whence it comes and where it goes. So is every one who has been born from the Spirit.‡

9. Nicodemus answered and said to him, How can these things be?

---

prevalent belief. The being born of "water and air" (ver. 5) perhaps has a physical allusion to natural, as well as to the deeper meaning of the supernatural life.

* The Sinaitic reads, "He cannot see the kingdom of the heavens."

† Literally, the air or breeze.

‡ "The believer shows by deed and word that an invisible influence has moved and inspired him."—*Dr. Westcott.*

10. Jesus answered and said to him, Art *thou* the teacher of Israel, and not aware of these things?

11. Verily, verily, I say unto you, That what we know,* we speak, and what we have seen we bear witness to, and our witness ye receive not.

12. If I told you things that happen on earth,† and ye believe not, how, if I shall have told you of things in heaven, will ye believe?

13. And no one has gone up to the heaven unless he who came down out of the heaven,‡ (even) the Son of Man.

14. And as Moses raised on high the serpent § in the wilderness, so must the Son of Man be raised on high,

---

* That is, Christ and his followers, perhaps including the evangelist (Dr. Westcott). The "we" is certainly a difficulty.

† As the invisible action of the wind.

‡ See the note on i. 52.

§ See viii. 28. The serpent (one of the many symbols of the productive power) was associated with healing, as it is represented twined round the staff of Esculapius. The symbol, as allowed by Moses, was not as *an idol*, but a charm, or fetish. The somewhat strained effort to find analogies or types of the crucifixion in the Old Testament is striking.

15. That every one who believes in him may have life everlasting.

16. For God so loved the world that he gave his Son, the Only-begotten,* that every one who believes on him may not perish but have life everlasting.†

17. For God sent not his Son into the world to judge the world, but that the world may be saved through him.

18. He that believes on him is not judged; he who believes not has been judged already for that he has not believed on the name of the Only-begotten Son of God.

19. And this judging‡ is because the light has come into the world, and (yet) men loved rather the darkness than the light, for their works were evil.

20. For every one who continues in evil

---

* See on i. 14. "In the historical Molekh worship of the Phœnicians an Only Son was regarded as the most acceptable offering to heaven" (Robert Brown, junr., F.S.A., "Eridanus," p. 22). In mythology, many of the "solar heroes" were Only Sons, as Jason, Achilles, and others enumerated in a remarkable passage, Hom. Od., xvi., 118.

† For the repetition see note on vi. 40.

‡ As in v. 22, etc., κρίσις may mean "separation" or "distinction."

deeds hates the light, and comes not to the light, that his works may not be brought to the proof.

21.* But he who does the truth comes to the light, that his works may be made manifest (and shown) to have been wrought in God.

22. After these (events) came Jesus and his disciples into the land of Judæa, and there he made a stay with them and baptised.

23. And there was John also, baptising at Ænon near Salim, because there were many water-pools there, and (the people) came and were baptised.

24. For John had not yet been cast into the prison.

25. There arose therefore a questioning on the part of the disciples of John with a Jew,† about purifying.‡

26. And they came to John and said to him,

---

* The Sinaitic omits the first part of this verse.

† The Sin. has "with Jews."

‡ There can be no doubt that a material *washing* was with the Jews, as well as with the early Greeks (see Iliad. i., 314), a rite regarded as efficacious in cleansing from sin, while again the commission of sin was held to be the cause of sickness (see v. 14). This explains chap. x. 11. Baptism was not as yet ordained as a Sacrament.

Rabbi, he who was with thee on the other side of the Jordan, to whom thou hast borne witness, behold, this man is baptising, and all are coming to him.

27. John answered and said, A man cannot receive anything unless it be given him out of heaven.

28. Ye do yourselves bear me witness that I said, *I* am not the Christ, but I have been sent* on a mission in advance of him.

29. He that has the bride is the bridegroom, but the friend of the bridegroom who stands and hears him rejoices with joy because of the bridegroom's voice. This joy therefore of mine has been fulfilled : †

30. It is for him to go on growing, and for me to be ever getting less.‡

31. He who comes from above is above all ; he that is of the earth *is* of the earth,§ and

---

* Gr., " But that I have been sent," etc.

† The joy of the faithful subordinate at the presence of the principal.

‡ Viz., in glory, renown, repute as Divine messengers. Again the language seems *solar*.

§ Our idiom is, "As he is of the earth, so he speaks of the earth."

of the earth he speaks; he that comes out of heaven is over all.*

32. What he has seen and heard, of that he bears witness, and his witness no one receives.

33. He who *has* received his witness sets his seal (to this), that God is true.

34. For he whom God sent utters the sayings of God; for he gives not by measure.†

35. The Father loves the Son and has given all things in(to) his hand.

36. He that believes‡ on the Son has life everlasting, but he who disobeys§ the Son shall not see life, but the wrath of God remains on him.

---

* The Beza gives, "He that comes out of heaven bears witness of what he has seen and heard;" the Sin., "Of him whom he has seen," etc.

† The Beza reads, "For not by measure does God give his Spirit;" and the Sin. has the same with "does he give."

‡ The Beza gives, "That he who believes in the Son may have," etc.; but the particle "that" is marked with dots as a doubtful reading.

§ Or "distrusts." The Sin. gives, "has not life."

IV.

1. WHEN therefore the Master had become aware that the Pharisees had heard that Jesus was making and baptising more disciples than John,*

2. (Albeit Jesus himself did not baptise, but his disciples),

3. He gave up Judæa, and went off into Galilee,

4. And he had to go through Samaria.

5. Accordingly he comes to a city of Samaria† called Sychar, near the plot of ground which Jacob had given to Joseph his son.

6. And it was there that Jacob's well was. Jesus therefore, being tired from the journey,

---

* The Vatican text has, apparently by mere error, "And John was (is) baptising." The ἤ, "than," is supplied by Sin. and Bez.

† The first clause of this verse is wanting in the Sinaitic, the sense being left imperfect.

sat down, just as he was, at the well; (the time) was about the sixth hour.

7. (Presently) there comes a woman from Samaria to draw water. Jesus says to her, Give me to drink.

8. For his disciples had gone off into the city to buy victuals.*

9. The woman of Samaria therefore says to him, How is it that *you*, being a Jew, ask of *me* to drink, who am a woman of Samaria? For the Jews have no friendly dealings with the Samaritans.†

10. Jesus answered and said to her, If thou hadst known the free gift of God, and who it is that says to thee, Give me to drink, thou wouldest have asked of him, and he would have given thee living water.

11. Says she to him, Master, you have no bucket, and the well is deep; whence then have you this living water? ‡

---

* "If they had been present they could have supplied the want."—*Dr. Westcott.*

† The Beza omits this sentence, together with the Sinaitic. Probably it was an ancient gloss.

‡ The woman understood "living" to mean fresh and sparkling from the spring, *vivos latices*. "This" (the) is omitted in B.

12. Surely *you* are not greater than our Father Jacob, who gave us the well, and himself drank from it, and his sons, and his cattle.

13. Jesus answered and said to her, Every one who drinks of this water shall thirst again.

14. But whosoever shall have drunk from the water which I will give him shall not thirst for all time, but the water which I will give him will become in him a fountain of water springing up into life everlasting.

15. Says the woman to him, Master, give me this water, that I may not thirst, nor come all the way to draw here.

16. He says to her, Go, call your husband, and come here.

17. The woman answered and said to him, I have no husband. Jesus says to her, You said well, I have no husband,

18. For you had five husbands, and he whom you have now is not your husband; this you have said truly.

19. Says the woman to him, Master, I perceive that you are a prophet.

20. Our fathers worshipped on this mountain,

and *ye* say that in Jerusalem is the place where one ought to worship.

21. Jesus says to her, Believe me, woman, that a time is coming when neither in this mountain nor in Jerusalem shall ye worship the Father.

22. *Ye* worship that which ye know not ; *we* worship that which we know, for that the (promised) salvation is from the Jews.

23. But the hour comes, and now is, when the real worshippers shall worship the Father in spirit and truth ; for the Father also seeks such for his worshippers.

24. God (is) a spirit, and they that worship him must worship in spirit and truth.*

25. Says the woman to him, I know that the Messiah is coming, who is called Christ ; when *he* shall have come, he will bring tidings of all things to us.

26. Jesus says to her, I am he who is talking to you.†

27. And at this came his disciples, and wondered that he was conversing with a

---

* The Sinaitic has, " in a spirit of truth."
† Compare ix. 37.

woman. Yet no one said, What seekest thou? or, Why dost thou talk with her?

28. The woman therefore left her water-pot, and went off into the city, and said to the people,

29. Come (and) see a man who told me all that (ever) I did; can it be that this is the Christ?

30. (Accordingly) they came forth from the city and began to come to him.

31. In the meanwhile the disciples kept asking him saying, Rabbi, eat.

32. But he said to them, I have meat to eat which *ye* know not of.

33. The disciples therefore said to each other, Can some one have brought him (something) to eat?

34. Says Jesus to them, *My* meat is that I should do the will of him who sent me, and complete his work.

35. Do not *ye* say that there is yet a space of four months, and the harvest is coming? Behold, I say to you, Lift up your eyes and observe how these tracts are white for harvest already.

36. He who reaps receives pay, and gathers

fruit for life everlasting,* that he who sows may rejoice together and he who reaps.

37. For in this (respect) the saying is true,† that there is one who sows and another who reaps.

38. I sent you to reap that which *ye* have not laboured at ;‡ others have toiled, and ye have entered into their toil.

39. And of that city many believed on him of the Samaritans, through the report of the woman who bare witness that he had told her all that she had (ever) done.

40. The people of Samaria therefore§ came to him (and) asked him to stay with them ; and he stayed there two days.

41. And many more believed through his word,

---

* That is, not for a temporary use. "Christ himself stands as the Lord of the harvest, and not here as the sower" (*Dr. Westcott*). The Beza here punctuates, "Already the reaper is getting pay."

† The Beza has, "For in this is the (or that) true saying ;" and so the Sinaitic.

‡ The Beza has, "I have sent you to reap ; *ye* toiled not ; others toiled," etc.

§ The Beza and Sinaitic read, "when therefore they asked him."

42. And they said to the woman, No longer do we believe through your talk,* for we ourselves have heard (him), and know that this is truly the Saviour of the world.†

43. And after the two days he went out thence into Galilee.

44. For Jesus himself bare witness ‡ that a prophet has not honour in his own country.

45. When therefore he had come into Galilee the Galilæans received him, having seen all that he had done in Jerusalem at the feast; for they had themselves also come to the feast.

46. He came therefore again to Cana of Galilee, where he had made the water wine. And there was (there) a man of the king's § court, whose son lay sick at Capharnaum.

47. This man having heard that Jesus had come out of Judæa into Galilee, went off to him,

---

* The Beza and Sinaitic give "through your evidence," or testimony.

† Meaning, perhaps, "The Messiah who will deliver the Jews from the Roman yoke." See, however, the wider sense in iii. 17. After "world" the Beza adds, "the Christ."

‡ That is, afforded a proof.

§ Viz., Herod Antipas, tetrarch of Galilee, who was popularly known as "King" (*Dr. Westcott*).

and besought him to come down* and heal his son, for he was about to die.

48. Jesus therefore said to him, Unless ye have seen signs and portents, ye will not believe.

49. The courtier says to him, Master, come down before my child dies.

50. Says Jesus to him, Go thy way, thy son lives. The man believed the word that Jesus had said to him, and went his way.

51. And as he was now going down (home), his servants met him, saying that his boy was alive.

52. He inquired of them therefore the hour at which he had taken a turn for the better. They said to him accordingly, Yesterday at the seventh hour the fever left him.

53. The father therefore knew that it was at that hour in which Jesus had said to him, Thy son lives. And he himself believed, and his whole household.

54. Now this is again the second sign that Jesus did after he had come out of Judæa into Galilee.

---

* Viz., to Capharnaum, to which there is a descent from the high land of Cana.

V.

1. AFTER these (events) there was a feast* of the Jews, and Jesus went up to Jerusalem.

2. Now there is at Jerusalem by the sheep-(gate) a plunging-bath which is called in Hebrew Bethsaida,† having five porches.

3. In these there were lying a number of the sick, blind, lame, shrivelled.‡

4. And there was a certain man there who for thirty-eight years had been in his infirmity.

6. Jesus having seen this man lying, and being aware that he had now been (infirm) for

---

* The Sinaitic reads "the feast."

† "Belzetha" the Beza, "Bethzatha" the Sinaitic, which has the remarkable reading, "There is at Jerusalem a bath for sheep," *i.e.*, a place used for sheep washing (*probatica piscina*, Vulgate). The spot has not been identified by modern research; it would seem to have been an intermittent spring, which they described as "troubled."

‡ The Beza adds, "paralytic, waiting for the movement of the water."

a long time, says to him, Do you wish to be cured?

7. The sick man answered him, Master, I have not (by me) a man, that, when the water is troubled, he may put me into the plunging-bath; but while *I* am coming, another before me goes down (into it).

8. Jesus says to him, Arise, take up thy pallet, and walk.

9. And immediately the man was cured,* and took up his bed and walked.

10. Now it was the Sabbath on that day. The Jews therefore said to him who had been healed, It is the Sabbath, and it is not lawful for you to take up (and carry) your pallet.

11. But he answered them, He who made me well, it was *he* that said to me, Take up your pallet and walk.

12. They asked him, Who *is* the man that said to you, Take up your pallet and walk?

13. But he who had been healed† knew not

---

* The Beza gives, "And the man was cured (became sound), and getting up he took up his pallet and walked; and it was (the) Sabbath." The Sinaitic, "The man became sound and got up and took up his pallet," etc.

† The Beza gives, "the infirm man knew not."

who it was; for Jesus had got away from the crowd that was on the spot.*

14. After these things Jesus finds him in the Temple; and he said to him, Behold, thou hast been cured; sin no more, lest something worse should happen to thee.†

15. The man went away and brought word to the Jews that it was Jesus who had made him well.

16. And it was on account of this (act) that the Jews persecuted‡ Jesus, because he had been doing these things on the Sabbath.

17. But he answered them, As my Father has been working till now, so I also continue (his) work.§

18. For this cause therefore the Jews sought still more to put him to death, because he was not only loosening (the obligation of) the

---

* Or, "there being a crowd." The Sin. reads, "in the midst."

† Between the commission of sin and the infliction of disease there was inseparable connection in the Jewish mind. Hence to say, "Thy sins are forgiven," was tantamount to saying, "Thy malady is cured."

‡ Or simply, "went in pursuit of," viz., to arrest him.

§ "My Father worketh even until now ("hitherto," A.V.), and I work" (R.V.). The above seems nearer our idiom.

Sabbath, but was also saying that God was his own Father, (thus) making himself equal to God.*

19. He answered therefore and said to them, Verily, verily I say unto you, the Son † can do nothing of himself, unless he beholds the Father doing something ; ‡ for whatever things *he* may do, these things the Son also does in like manner.

20. For the Father loves the Son, and shews him all things which he himself does ; and greater works than these will he shew him, that ye may marvel.§

21. For as the Father raises the dead and quickens them, so also the Son quickens whom he wills.

22. For not even the Father ¶ judges any one,

---

* Compare x. 33. † The Beza adds, " of man."

‡ Initiating, as it were, some work, which the Son, having the same will with the Father, *carries out*. The words *may* be taken as a denial of the charge, ἴσον σεαυτὸν ποιεῖς. In the patriarchal family, the dutiful and trusted son follows and aids the action of the father, without claiming to be one with him except in will.

§ That wonder, and in consequence belief, may be excited in you, who now question my authority (*Dr. Westcott*).

¶ That is, though invested with supreme authority.

but the judging he has given entirely to the Son,

23. That all may honour the Son even as they honour the Father. He that honours not the Son does not honour the Father who sent him.

24. Verily, verily I say unto you, that he who hears my word and has faith in him who sent me, has life everlasting, and comes not into judgment, but has passed out of the death into the life.

25. Verily, verily I say unto you, that the hour is coming and now is when the dead shall hear the voice of the Son of God, and those who hear (it) shall live.*

---

* The Sin. reads, "and having heard shall live." Unless "the dead" and "all who are in the tombs" (ver. 28) means those who are morally and spiritually dead and buried in their sins, these words must be taken to affirm the early return of Christ, and the rousing of the (sleeping) dead by a loud call (1 Thess. iv. 16), or the equally inconceivable summons of the notes of a trumpet,—a figure of speech borrowed from the military phrase, the ὄρθιος νόμος, or " rousing strain," but taken literally rather than figuratively in 1 Cor. xv. 52, and elsewhere. It is by a *loud* voice that Lazarus was recalled to life, xi. 43. The same idea prevailed in invoking the spirits of the dead, Æsch., *Pers.*, 687 ; Virg., Æn., iii., 67.

26. For as the Father * has life in himself, so to the Son also he gave to have life in himself,

27. And he gave him authority to hold judgment, because he is Son of Man.

28. Marvel not at this, that (I said)† the hour is coming in which all who are in the tombs shall hear his voice,

29. And come forth; those who have done good into the resurrection of life, and those who have practised the things that are evil into the resurrection of judgment.

30. *I* can do nothing of myself; as I hear, (so) I give judgment; and this sentence of mine is just, because I do not seek my own will, but the will of him who sent me.

31. If I bear witness about myself, my witness is not (accepted as) true.

32. There is another who bears witness

---

* The Beza has "the living Father." The Sinaitic reading is peculiar, "As the Father has life in himself, and gave to him judgment to exercise power."

† "Fo the hour is coming (cometh)." A. and R.V. But the statement in ver. 25 is repeated, though with some variety of expression. For "judgment" (κρίσις, see on iii. 19.

about me, and I know* that the witness which he bears about me is true.

33. *Ye* have dispatched (messengers) to John, and he has borne witness to the truth.

34. But *I* do not take my testimony from man; but these things I say that you may be saved.†

35. *He* was that torch that burns and gives light, and ye were willing to exult for a season in his light.

36. But I have a testimony greater than John's; for the works which the Father has given me to complete,—(yea), the very works that I do,—bear witness about me, that it is the Father who has sent me.

37. And the Father that sent me, he it is that has borne witness about me, (though) as yet ye have neither heard his voice nor seen his form.

38. And his word ye have not abiding in

---

* The Beza and Sinaitic read, " and ye know."
† I do not appeal to John, but to him who sent me, in order that even the unbelieving Jew may have a share in the coming salvation.

you, because whom he sent, in him ye have no faith.

39. Ye search the Scriptures, because *ye* think ye have in them life everlasting; and (though) they are (the writings) that bear witness about me,

40. Yet* ye care not to come to me that ye may have life.†

41. Glory from *men* I receive not.

42. But well do I know that *ye* have not in yourselves the love of God ‡

43. *I* have come in my Father's name, and (yet) ye receive me not. If another should come in his own name, him ye will receive.

44. How can *ye* have faith, when ye receive glory from each other, and seek not that glory that comes from the Only one ?§

45. Think not that *I* will accuse you to the

---

* Greek, "and ye will not," etc. Dr. Westcott says, "There is a deep pathos in the simple co-ordination *and* . . . *and*." But it hardly corresponds with our idiom.

† The Beza gives, "life everlasting."

‡ "The Jews had not the love of God, and their rejection of Christ was the sign of the fatal defect" (*Dr. Westcott*).

§ The Beza and Sinaitic give "from the only God," and so R.V.

Father; there is (another) who accuses you to the Father, (even) Moses, on whom ye have put your hope.

46. For if ye had faith in Moses ye would have faith in me; for it was about me that he wrote.*

47. But if ye believe not his writings, how do ye believe † my sayings?

---

* If Christ really said this, it was consistent with his plain avowal that he was the Messiah, iv. 26. But everywhere in the New Testament an effort is shown to make the Old Testament distinctly prophetic of Christ. It is not unlikely that, to give weight and authority to an opinion so fondly cherished by his followers, words were attributed to him which seem at variance with his usual policy of concealment.

† The Beza gives, "how should you (Sin., shall you) believe," etc.

VI.

1. AFTER these (events) Jesus went away to the other side of the Sea of Galilee, that (called) Tiberias.

2. And a great crowd went with him, for they had been watching* the signs which he did on those that were sick.

3. And Jesus went up† into the mountain and sat there with his disciples;

4. And the Passover, the feast of the Jews, was nigh.

5. Jesus therefore having lifted up his eyes and seen that a great crowd was coming to him, says to Philip, Whence are we to buy loaves, that these may eat?

6. (Now this he said by way of trying him, for he knew himself what he intended to do.)

---

* Observing, beholding, gazing at. "For they saw," Sin.
† The Sinaitic reads "went off," with the Beza.

7. Philip answered him, Loaves costing two hundred denars* are not enough for them, that each may get a little.

8. Says one of the disciples to him,—Andrew, the brother of Simon Peter,—

9. There is a lad here, who has five barley loaves and two pieces of fish ;† but what are these to so many?

10. Said Jesus, Make the people recline.‡ Now there was much grass§ in the place. The men accordingly reclined, in number about five thousand.

11. Jesus therefore took the loaves, and having given thanks he distributed them to those who were reposing,‖ likewise also of the pieces of fish, as much as they would.

12. And when they were filled, he says to

---

* About as many francs.

† Or simply "fish," as expressed in Matthew and Mark. See on xxi. 9. See Athenæus, ix., p. 385, E.

‡ The position assumed by Easterns, as by Greeks and Romans, at meals;—not "sitting," but lying back with the head propped.

§ Properly, herbage or pasturage for cattle.

‖ The Beza reads, "And gave thanks and gave (them) to his disciples, and the disciples to those reposing (lying back)."

his disciples, Collect the broken portions that are left over, that nothing may be lost.

13. Accordingly they collected them, and filled twelve hampers* with the scraps from the five barley loaves, which remained over to those who had eaten.

14. The people therefore having seen what signs† he had done, began to say, This is truly the prophet that was to come into the world.

15. Jesus therefore, being aware that they were about to come and carry him off to make him a king, retreated back again to the mountain alone by himself.‡

16. Now when evening had come his disciples went down to the sea,

17. And entering a boat proceeded to the other side of the sea to Capharnaum. And dusk by this time had come on,§ and Jesus had not yet come to them,

18. And the sea, as a great wind was blowing, began to be stirred.

---

* Or " stout baskets " (Dr. Westcott).
† The Beza has " what sign," or, " the sign which," etc.
‡ The Beza adds, " and there prayed."
§ The Sinaitic and Beza read, " and the dusk had overtaken them, and," etc.

19. When therefore they had rowed some twenty-five or thirty furlongs, they behold Jesus walking on the sea,* and getting near the boat, and they were afraid.

20. But he says to them, It is I, be not any more afraid.

21. They were willing therefore to take him into the boat, and straightway the boat was at the land for which they were making.

22. On the morrow the crowd that stood on the other side of the sea saw that no other boat was there, but one only ;† and that Jesus had not entered with his disciples into the boat, but his disciples had gone off without him.‡

23. But boats had come from Tiberias, near the spot where they had eaten the bread after the Master had blessed it.

24. When therefore the crowd saw that Jesus

---

* Of this miraculous power there are examples in mythology, *e.g.*, Apoll. Rhod., i., 182 ; Virg., Æn., vii., 810.

† The Sinaitic and Beza read, "except that one into which the disciples of Jesus had embarked."

‡ The verb is omitted in the Sin., which continues thus : "When therefore the boats had come up from Tiberias which was near, where also they had ate the bread ;" the Beza, "Other boats having come from Tiberias near the place where," etc., omitting "after the Master had blessed it."

was not there, nor his disciples, they got into the boats themselves* and came to Capharnaum seeking Jesus.

25. And [not] having found† him on the other side of the sea, they said to him, Rabbi, when camest thou here?

26. Jesus answered them and said, Verily, verily I say to you, Ye seek me,‡ not because ye saw signs,§ but because ye did eat of the loaves and were filled.

27. Work not (at) the food that perishes, but (at) the food that remains unto life everlasting, which the Son of Man shall give you.‖ For him the Father did seal,¶ (even) God.

28. They said therefore to him, What must we do that we may work the works of God?"**

---

* The Beza reads, "they got boats for themselves."
† The negative must be from an error, unless the sense meant was, "seeking and not having found him." It is wanting in the Beza and Sinaitic.
‡ This verb is omitted in the Sin.
§ The Beza adds, "and wonders."
‖ The Sin. has "offers you," with the Beza.
¶ The Sin. omits this verb, making the sense "For him the Father, even God, (gives to you)."
** The Beza has, "What must we work at that we may do," etc.

29. Jesus answered and said to them, This is the work of God, that ye may believe on him whom he sent.

30. They said therefore to him, What then dost *thou* do as a sign that we may see and believe thee? What *is* thy work?

31. Our fathers ate the manna in the wilderness, even as it is written, Bread* out of heaven he gave them to eat.

32. Jesus then said to them, Verily, verily I say unto you, It was not Moses who gave you the bread out of heaven, but it is my Father who gives you that bread out of heaven which is the real bread.

33. For the bread of God is that which comes down out of heaven, and gives life to the world.

34. They said therefore to him, Master, at all times and seasons give us this bread.

35. Said Jesus to them, *I* am the bread of life; he that comes to me shall not hunger, and he who has faith in me shall not at any time thirst.

---

* " Bread " is omitted in the Sin.

36. But I told *you* that ye have even seen me,* and yet ye have not faith.

37. All that the Father gives me shall come to me, and him who comes to me I will not cast out.

38. For I have come down from heaven not that I may do my own will, but the will of him who sent me.

39. And this is the will of him who sent me,† that of all that he has given to me I should not lose anything, but should raise it up on the last day.

40. For this is the will of my Father, that every one who beholds the Son and has faith in him may have life everlasting, and that *I* should raise him upon the last day.‡

41. The Jews then murmured about him, because he had said, I am the bread that has come down out of heaven.

---

* That is, "doing signs," ver. 30.

† The first clause of this verse is omitted in the Sin.

‡ The repetitions in this chapter are so remarkable and so frequent, that it reads like a collection of sayings attributed, with slight varieties, to Jesus in conversation at different times with his disciples. These may have been faithfully stored and collected, but not skilfully put together.

42. And they said, Is not this man Jesus the son of Joseph, whose father we know, and his mother?* How is it that he now says, I am come down out of heaven?

43. Jesus answered and said to them, Murmur not with each other.

44. No one can come to me unless my Father who sent me shall have drawn him; and I will raise him up on the last day.

45. It is written in the Prophets, And they shall all be taught of God. Every one who hath heard from the Father and learnt, cometh to me.

46. Not that any one has seen the Father, except him who is from God; he *has* seen the Father.†

47. Verily, verily I say to you, He that has faith ‡ has life everlasting.

48. *I* am that Bread of Life.

49. Your fathers ate the manna in the wilderness, and they died.

---

* The Sin. reads, "whose father also we know," omitting "and his mother."

† The Sin. reads, "seen God."

‡ The Beza adds, "in me."

50. This is the bread which comes down (to you) out of heaven, that a man may eat of it and not die.

51. *I* am that Living Bread that came down out of heaven. If a man eats of this bread,* he shall live for ever; yea, and the bread which *I* will give him is my flesh for the life of the world.†

52. The Jews therefore contended with each other saying, How can this man give us his flesh to eat?

53. Jesus therefore said to them, Verily, verily I say unto you, Unless ye eat ‡ the flesh of the Son of Man and drink his blood, ye have no life§ in yourselves.

54. He that eats my flesh ‖ and drinks my blood has life everlasting, and I will raise him up on the last day.

---

* The ἄρτος ὁ ἐπιούσιος, "the bread that comes to us," of the Lord's Prayer. The Sin. reads, "of my bread."

† The Sin. reads, "the bread which I will give for the life of the world is my flesh." Christ seems to speak of himself as the Paschal Lamb.

‡ The Beza reads, "Unless ye shall have received."

§ The Sin. reads, "life everlasting;" the Beza, "the life."

‖ The Beza reads, "his flesh and drinks his blood." Nothing can be more remarkable than the oft-repeated assertion (fifteen

55. For my flesh is true meat and my blood is true drink.*

56. He that eats my flesh and drinks my blood abides in me as I do in him.†

57. Even as the living Father sent me, and I live through the Father, so he also who eats me, *he* (I say) shall live through me.

---

times in this one chapter) of precisely the same thing. Looking to the context, and the nature of the case, the obvious conclusion is, that the language used must be purely and wholly figurative and spiritual. Yet it is clear that, from the first, a material act conveying a spiritual efficacy has been understood to have been intended and commanded as a precept.

Christ's promises of his speedy return, or Second Coming, were, in the very same way, taken literally; yet they were not fulfilled by the result, nor was that which is so explicitly declared in i. 52.

Dr. Westcott holds that John vi. does not refer primarily, nor even prophetically, to the Eucharist, but that the latter was the "concrete form" of a truth which here is enunciated absolutely.

To the Greek, who was familiar with the Bacchic (Oriental) orgies in the rending and devouring ($\tau\rho\omega\gamma\epsilon\iota\nu$, v. 54) raw flesh in a religious frenzy, the phraseology in the Gospel would appear less startling than it is to us. See Eur., *Bacch.*, 139. But Christ, speaking as himself a Jew, naturally has in mind the consumption of the flesh of the lamb at the Passover.

* The Sin. has, "For my flesh truly is drink."

† The Beza adds, "Even as the Father in me and I in the Father. Verily, verily I say unto you, Unless you receive the body of the Son of Man, as the bread of life, ye have not life in him." In 57 it has, "he who receives me, he also lives," etc.

58. *This** is the bread that came down out of heaven; it is not as your fathers ate and died; (for) he that eats *this* bread shall live for ever.

59. These things he said at a meeting† (of the Jews) as he taught at Capharnaum.

60. Many therefore of his disciples having heard him said, Hard is this saying; who can listen to it?

61. But Jesus knowing in himself ‡ that his disciples were murmuring about this, said to them, Does this scandalise you?

62. (What) then if ye should behold the Son of Man ascending where he was before?

63. The Spirit it is that quickeneth; the flesh profits nothing. The sayings that I have spoken to you are spirit and are life.

64. But there are some of you who have not faith. For Jesus § knew from the first who

---

* The Sinaitic omits "this."

† The Beza reads, "the meeting (or synagogue)," and adds "on the Sabbath."

‡ The Beza has, "When therefore Jesus knew that his disciples were murmuring among themselves."

§ The Sin. reads "For the Saviour," and, "who they were (are) that have faith."

they were that had not faith, and who it was that was about to betray him.

65. And he said, For this I have told you, that no one can come to me unless it be given him from the Father.

66. Upon this many of his disciples went back, and no longer walked with him.

67. Jesus therefore said to the Twelve, Are *ye* also minded to go away?

68. Simon Peter answered him, Master, to whom shall we depart? Thou hast sayings of everlasting life, and we have believed, and are convinced that thou art the Holy one of God.

69. Jesus answered them, Did not I choose out for myself you, the Twelve, and one of you is a slanderer * (of me)?

70. Now he spoke of Judas, (the son) of Simon Iscariot,† for he it was who was about to betray him, being one of the Twelve.

---

* Judas *misrepresented* Christ, in telling the priests falsehoods about his teaching. The common version, "one of you is a devil," seems in every way objectionable.

† The Sin. reads, "from Caryotus" ("a man of Kerioth," *Westcott*).

VII.

1. AND after these events Jesus walked* in Galilee, for he was unwilling to walk in Judæa, because the Jews were seeking to put him to death.

2. Now the feast of the Jews was nigh, (that called) the Fixing of the Tents.†

3. Accordingly his brethren said to him, Leave these parts‡ and go into Judæa, that thy disciples also may behold the works that thou art doing.

4. For no man does a thing in secret, and seeks that it§ should be talked about. If thou doest these (works), show thyself plainly to the world.

---

* That is, went about teaching.
† The feast of the Tabernacles, in commemoration of the life in the wilderness.
‡ Lit., "Make a change from this place (to another)."
§ The Sinaitic has, "that he himself," etc.

5. (For not even his own brethren were as yet disposed to put faith in him.)

6. Jesus therefore says to them, *My* time has not yet arrived; but *your* time is always present (and) ready.*

7. The world cannot hate *you;* but me it does hate, for that I bear witness about it that its deeds are evil.

8. Go ye (therefore) up to the feast; *I* go not up as yet to *this* feast,† because *my* time is not yet fully come.‡

9. And having said these (words) to them, he remained § in Galilee.

10. But when his brethren had gone up to the feast, then he also went up himself, not openly, but as if in secret. ‖

11. The Jews therefore¶ made search for him at the feast, and kept saying, Where is that man?

---

* The Beza and Sin. read, "is always ready."

† That is, not till the later feast of the Passover. The context shows the meaning to be, "I do not *accompany* you; do you go alone."

‡ Lit., "has not been filled up" (of the proper number of months and days).

§ The Sin. and Beza have, "he himself remained."

‖ The Sin. and Beza give, "not openly, but in secret."

¶ That is, seeing his brethren had arrived.

12. And there was much murmuring about him among the crowds,* (and) some said, He is a good man, while others said, No, he is deceiving the multitude.

13. Yet no one spoke freely about him through fear of the Jews.†

14. But when the feast was now at the middle Jesus went up into the temple and began to teach.

15. The Jews thereupon were surprised, saying, How (comes it that) this man knows letters, not having learnt them?

16. Jesus therefore answered them and said, My teaching is not mine, but his who sent me.

17. If any man desire to do *his* will, he will have right judgment ‡ about the teaching, whether it is from God, or I am speaking from myself.

18. He that speaks from himself seeks his

---

* The *circuli*, or knots of talkers. The Beza reads, "among the common people."

† That is, they feared to praise him, or to seem to take part with him.

‡ Lit. "he will (be able to) form a conviction about," etc.

own glory,* but he that seeks the glory of him that sent him, that man is true,† and there is no dishonesty in him.

19. Did not Moses give you the law, and (is it not that) not one of you acts on the law? Why are ye seeking to put *me* to death? ‡

20. The crowd answered, Thou art possessed ; who wants to put thee to death?

21. Jesus answered and said to them, One work I did, and ye are all wondering on account of that.§

22 Moses (himself) hath given you the (rite of) circumcision,—not that it is from Moses, but (rather) from your forefathers,‖— and on the Sabbath ye circumcise a man.

23. If that man receives circumcision on the Sabbath, in order that the law of Moses may

---

* That is, credit, or repute.

† Or "sincere," "truthful," not acting on self-interest (so in Rom., II., xii., 433).

‡ Perhaps, τί ἐμὲ ζητεῖτε, etc. (emphatic).

§ Th Beza has a full stop after "wondering." "For this cause ath Moses given" (R.V., with "marvel because of this" i the note. The Sin. omits "because of this").

‖ In ts origin it was a pagan rite, and in all probability "phall." The notion of making "a *part* of a man all right"s easily explained on this view.

not be broken, are ye angry with *me* for making a whole man* sound on the Sabbath?

24. Judge not according to appearance, but give the judgment that is just.

25. Some persons therefore from Jerusalem began to say, Is not this he whom they are seeking to put to death?

26. And lo! he is speaking plainly and they say nothing to him. Can it be that the rulers had truly concluded that this is the Christ?

27. But we know about this man, whence *he* is; but when the Christ comes, no man knows whence he is.†

28. Jesus therefore spoke with a loud voice teaching in the temple, and saying, Both me ye know, and whence I am ye know, and (that) I have not come of myself, but he who sent me is the true ‡ (God), whom ye know not.

---

* Not merely a *part* or member, but the entire man. See v. 9. The rendering, "every whit whole," is undobtedly erroneous. Such a rendering is utterly opposed to the laws of the Greek language. The Latin of the Beza is right, "Quod totum hominem sanum feci in sabbato;" and so the Vlgate.

† The Messiah is simply "sent."

‡ The Sin. reads "is true" (ἀληθής, not ἀληθινός).

29. I *do* know him (and) that * I am from him, and that he sent me.

30. They sought therefore to take him by force, and (yet) no man laid his hand on him, because his hour had not yet come.

31. But of the common people † many had faith in him, and they kept saying, When the Christ comes, will he do more signs than those which this man has done?

32. (Now) the Pharisees heard the people muttering about him in these words, and the chief priests and the Pharisees dispatched men under their orders to take him by force.‡

33. Thereupon Jesus said, Yet a little while I am with you, and (then) I depart to him that sent me.§

34. Ye shall seek me and ye shall not find me, and where I am, there ye are not able to come.

35. The Jews therefore said to themselves,

---

* "Because I am from him" (R.V.); "That I am with him" (Sin.)

† The "mob," "multitude," "the masses," as we say. See on ver. 46.

§ Many such expressions are intelligible only on the view, that Jesus believed himself to be (not God, but) the Messiah.

Where *is* this man about to go, that we shall not find him? Is it to the dispersed Greeks * that he is about to go, and to teach the Greeks? †

36. What means this word which he spoke, Ye shall seek me and ye shall not find me, and, Where I am ye are not able to come?

37. Now on the last day, the great one of the feast,‡ Jesus stood and said in a loud voice, If any one thirst, let him come to me and drink.

38. If any one believes on me, as the Scripture saith, there shall flow out of his belly rivers of living water.

39. (Now this he said concerning the Spirit, which those who had faith in him were about to receive; for not as yet had the Holy Spirit been given,§ because Jesus was not yet glorified.)

40. (Some) therefore of the multitude having

---

* Lit., "the dispersion of the Hellenes," *i.e.*, the Jews, in the various Roman provinces.

† Withdrawing himself from further teaching among his Jewish brethren.

‡ The Beza reads, "on the great day, the last one of the feast," and "let him who believes, etc., drink: rivers," etc.

§ "For as yet there was not a Spirit" (Sin.)

heard these words, kept saying, that "This is of a truth the Prophet."

41. Others said, This is the Christ, while others said, Why, surely *the Christ* comes not out of Galilee?

42. Saith not the Scripture that the Christ comes of the seed of David,* and that from Bethlehem, the village where David was, cometh the Christ?

43. Thereupon there arose a schism among the people because of him.

44. And some of them wanted to take him by force, but no man laid his hands upon him.

45. Accordingly, the men under orders came to the high priests and the Pharisees; and they said to them, Why did ye not bring him?

46. Those under their orders † replied, Never did man ‡ so speak.

---

* Hence the pedigrees in Matthew and Luke have as their object to show that Christ, as the Messiah, was really descended from David, though through different lines.

† The word ὑπηρέται, commonly rendered "officers," is the term used in this Gospel for subordinates, those acting at the instance and command of superiors.

‡ No *mere* man, *i.e.*, we did not bring him because he seemed to us the Messiah. The Beza adds, "as this man speaks;" and so the Sin.

47. Thereupon the Pharisees answered, Surely *ye* likewise have not been led astray?

48. Did any one of the rulers put faith in him, or of the Pharisees?

49. [Not so]; but this rabble, that knows not the law,* are under a curse.†

50. Says Nicodemus to them,—he that had come to him before,‡ being one of them,§

51. Surely our law doth not pass sentence on the man (accused), unless (the judge) shall have first heard from himself, and be acquainted with what he is doing? ‖

52. They answered and said to him, Perhaps thou art thyself too from Galilee! ¶ Search, and see (for thyself) that out of Galilee no prophet is to arise.

---

* Illiterate, and without critical knowledge of what the prophets do say of the Messiah.

† Or, " cursed as they are " (lit., " they are accursed ").

‡ The Beza has, " he who had come to him at night at the first." The Sinaitic omits this clause.

§ That is, a Pharisee, and a ruler, iii. 1.

‖ The Beza reads, "and what he did shall have become known."

¶ That is, zealous for the credit of your country.

VIII.

12. AGAIN therefore Jesus spoke to them saying, I am the light of the world; he who goes with me shall not walk in the dark, but shall have the light of life.*

13. Thereupon the Pharisees said to him, *Thou* art bearing witness about thyself; thy witness is not true.

14. Jesus answered and said to them, Even if I do bear witness about myself, my witness is true, because I know whence I came and where I am going to; but ye know not whence I come or where I am going to.

15. Ye judge according to the flesh; I judge no man,

16. And even if I should judge, this judg-

---

* The Sin. reads, "but has," etc. The narrative of the woman taken in adultery, forming the first eleven verses of this chapter, with the last of the preceding, are wanting in the Vatican and Sinaitic, but are given, with some variations from the received readings, in the Beza.

ment of mine is true,* because I am not alone, but I and the Father who sent me (judge).†

17. And it is even written in your own law, that of two men the testimony is true.

18. I am he that gives testimony about myself, and the Father who sent me gives testimony about *me*.

19. They said to him therefore, Where is thy Father? Jesus answered, Neither me do ye know nor my Father: if ye had known me, ye would have known my Father also.

20. These sayings he spoke in the Treasury, as he taught in the temple;‡ and no man laid hands on him§ because his hour had not yet come.

21. He said to them therefore a second time, I am going away and ye shall seek me, and in your sin ye shall die. Where I go, ye cannot come.

22. The Jews therefore began to say,‖ Surely

---

* Lit., a genuine, real, unbiassed judgment, not partial nor one-sided.

† The figure of speech seems borrowed from the assessor or πάρεδρος, who takes a part in giving a judicial sentence.

‡ The latter clause is omitted in the Sinaitic.

§ Viz., on the charge of blasphemy.

‖ The imperfect ἔλεγον is occasionally (as here in the Beza)

he is not going to kill himself, that he says, Where I go, ye cannot come?

23. And he said to them, Ye are of those below, I am of those above; ye are of this world, I am not of this world.

24. Therefore said I to you, That ye shall die in your sins; for unless ye believe that I Am,* ye *will* die in your sins.

25. They began therefore to say to him, Who art thou? Jesus said to them, What I even tell you (I was) in the beginning.

26. Many things I have to say about you and to judge; but he who sent me is true, and (the words) I heard from him,† these speak I unto the world.‡

---

written ἔλεγαν, and it is a question whether, as the usual aorist ἔλεξαν is not used in this Gospel, the writer did not intend it for a form of the second aorist. Assuming it to be the imperfect, we have commonly rendered it "they began to say," or "they kept saying."

* The writer appears to understand this as an assertion of identity with the Logos. With τὴν ἀρχὴν (25) compare ἐν ἀρχῇ ἦν ὁ Λόγος (i. 1). This pre-existence seems implied under the formula "I am." The suggestion in the note (R.V.), "How is it that I even speak to you at all?" is of no value.

† The Sin. has, "with him," and "the Father who sent me."

‡ The full meaning would seem to be, ("The world may not believe me,) but what I tell the world is the truth, which I received from the Father himself."

27. They were not aware* that he was speaking to them of the Father.

28. Jesus therefore said,† When ye have raised the Son of Man on high,‡ then shall ye know that I Am,§ and that I do nothing of myself, but even as the Father taught me, so I speak.

29. And he that sent me is with me ; he did not leave me by myself, because I do what is pleasing to him at all times.

30. On his saying these (words), many believed in him.

31. Jesus therefore said ‖ to those Jews who had trust in him, If *ye* abide in this my word, ye are truly my disciples ;

32. And ye shall know¶ the truth, and that truth will set you free.

---

* That is, " They said they were not," or " He observed they were not aware," and therefore he said, etc. The Beza reads, "that he calls God his Father;" the Sinaitic, "that he spoke to them of God as his Father," or " told them that God was his Father."

† The Beza and Sinaitic add, " again to them."

‡ See iii. 14.

§ My existence from the first (24). See on 58.

‖ Or, "went on to say " (imperfect).

¶ Or, " become acquainted with."

33. They replied to him, We are the seed of Abraham, and have never yet been slaves to any one; how is it that *thou* sayest, Ye shall become free?

34. Jesus answered them, Verily, verily I say unto you, that *every* one who committeth the sin* is the slave of that sin.†

35. Now the slave does not remain in the family for all time; the son does remain for all time.‡

36. If therefore the son shall have given you freedom, ye shall be free indeed.

37. I know that ye are the seed of Abraham; but ye seek to put me to death because this word of mine hath not free course in you.§

38. What I have seen with the Father‖ I

---

* Or, in our idiom, "some particular sin," or even sin in the abstract. Compare 1 John 3, 4, πᾶς ὁ ποιῶν τὴν ἁμαρτίαν καὶ τὴν ἀνομίαν ποιεῖ.

† The Beza reads, "is a slave."

‡ In a patriarchal house; with an allusion to the Roman practice of emancipating slaves, and making them *liberti*, "really and legally free." The Sin. omits the last clause.

§ So R.V.; "hath no place in you," A.V.; "non capit in vobis," Beza and Vulgate. The true meaning is uncertain.

‖ As the eternal Logos, or "I Am."

speak; do ye therefore also what ye heard*
from (your) father.†

41. They answered and said to him, *Our
father is Abraham.* Says Jesus to them, If ye
are (really) the children of Abraham, ye would
do the works of Abraham.‡

40. But as it is, ye are seeking to put me to
death, a man who has spoken to you the truth
which I heard from God. This Abraham did
not do.

41. *Ye* are doing the works of *your* father.
They said to him, *We* were not born of forni-
cation; we have one Father, our God.

42. Said Jesus to them, If God were your
Father, ye would love§ me; for I came forth

---

* The Beza has, "what ye have seen with your father;" the Sinaitic, "what ye have seen from your father."

† That is, follow the teaching of Abraham, of whom you say you are the seed; ("and ye also do," R. V., but with note as above).

‡ It is exceedingly probable that the true reading is the imperative ποιεῖτε, not the imperfect ἐποιεῖτε, which gives a syntax that is hardly Greek. The three MSS. here agree. The A.V. follows Stephen's text, "If ye were (ἦτε, not ἐστε) Abraham's children, ye would do," etc. The context requires, "If ye *are* his children, act according to his precepts."

§ Or, "be devotedly attached to me."

from God and am come (into the world)*; for think not that I have come of myself, but it was he that sent me.†

43. Why will ye not understand what I am now saying to you?‡ (It is) because ye cannot hear this my word.

44. *Ye* are of your father the devil, and the lusts of your father ye desire to go on doing.§ *He* was a man-slayer from the first,‖ and he stands not in the truth, because truth is not in him. When (one) utters that which is a falsehood, he is speaking from his own, because he is a liar, and (so is) his father.¶

---

* Possibly the writer meant, "and return to him." This is not the classical use of ἥκω, but, on the other hand, the future ἥξω regularly means "I will return," in the best writers.

† Again he plainly affirms that he is the Messiah. ("For neither have I come," R. V.)

‡ Literally, "Why do ye not make yourselves acquainted with this speech (talk) of mine." The Beza has, "this truth of mine."

§ This is the force of the present infinitive ("it is your will to do," R. V.).

‖ Viz., as shown by the action of Cain.

¶ Or, "as his father (the devil) also is." The passage is difficult and obscure. It seems best to supply τις, as the subject of λαλῇ, or ὃς ἂν may have been corrupted to ὅταν. The common rendering, "he is a liar and the father of it," is objectionable from the use of the article (ὁ πατήρ) with the

45. But because *I* speak the truth, ye believe me not.

46. Which of you can bring a charge against me of sin? If I speak the truth, why do ye not believe me?*

47. He that is of God heareth the words of God; it is for this that *ye* hear (them) not, because ye are not of God.

48. The Jews answered and said to him, Say we not well that thou art a Samaritan, and art possessed?

49. Jesus answered, I am not possessed, but I honour my Father and ye dishonour me.

50. But it is not I that seek my glory; there is one who seeks and judges.†

51. Verily, verily I say unto you, If a man keep my word, he will not behold death for all time.‡

---

predicate. If proof could be found that any of the old theologies attributed a father to the devil (as a phrase still survives, "the devil's dam"), then αὐτοῦ would refer to διαβόλου, and ver. 44 would more naturally mean, as Greek, "ye are of the devil's father," etc.

* This verse (46) and the end of 47 are omitted in the Beza.

† My Father seeks that honour should be paid to one whom he sent (54), and judges those who refuse it (see iii. 18).

‡ "He shall never see death" (A. and R. V.).

52. Said the Jews unto him, Now we are sure that thou art possessed. Abraham is dead, and the prophets, and *thou* sayest, If any one keep my word he will not behold * death for all time.

53. Surely thou art not greater than our father Abraham, who is dead? The prophets too are dead; whom makest thou thyself?

54. Jesus answered, If I glorify † myself, my glory is nought; it is my Father that glorifies me, of whom ye say that he is your God,

55. And (yet) ye know him not. But I know him, and if I should say that I do not know him, I shall be like unto you, a liar; but I do know him, and his word I keep.

56. Abraham your father rejoiced ‡ to see this my day, and he saw it, § and was glad.

57. The Jews then said to him, Thou art not yet fifty years old, and hast thou seen Abraham? ||

---

* The Sin. and Beza read "taste."

† Or, "give credit to."

‡ Literally, "put himself into a state of delight," or exultation.

§ Viz., in assurance and faith, or in some supposed revelation of the Logos to him.

|| The Sinaitic reads, "and Abraham hath seen thee," or, "and hath," etc.

58. Said Jesus unto them, Verily, verily I say unto you, before Abraham was born, I Am.*

59. Thereupon they took up stones to throw at him, (but) Jesus hid himself,† and (afterwards) went out of the temple.

---

* This was the reply to the question of the high priest. Mark xiv. 62, "Art thou the Christ?" and it is taken to mean "Yes, I am." But, as a formula, ἐγώ εἰμι may bear a deeper meaning (see ver. 28, and xiii. 19).

† Or, "was withdrawn from sight,"—meaning perhaps, in some mysterious way. The Vulgate and Beza have, "abscondit se."

IX.

1. AND in passing on he saw a man (who had been) blind from birth.*

2. And his disciples asked him saying, Rabbi, who sinned, this man or his parents, that he should have been born blind?

3. Jesus answered, Neither did this man sin, nor his parents; but (this was done) that the works of God might be made manifest in him.

4. *We* must be working the works of him that sent me,† while it is day; the night is coming, when no man *can* work.

5. When I am in the world, I am the light of the world. ‡

6. Having said this he spit on the ground,

---

* The Beza adds, "sitting (there)."
† The Sinaitic reads, that "sent us."
‡ See i. 7—9.

and made mud * out of the spittle, and put the mud from it on the (man's) eyes,

And said to him, Go and wash in the bathing-pool of Siloam, which is interpreted to mean " Sent."† He went away seeing.‡

8. The neighbours therefore, and those who had been used to see him before, that he was a beggar, began to say, Is not this he that sat and begged?

9. Some said, It is he; others said, No, but he is like him. He said, I am the man.

10. Accordingly they said to him, How were your eyes opened?

11. He answered, The man that is called Jesus made some mud and plastered over my eyes, and said to me, Go to Siloam and wash thyself. Accordingly having gone away and washed myself I recovered my sight.

---

* Thus Plato (" Theæt.," p. 147, c.) defines the word, which is commonly rendered " clay," meaning simply " wet earth."

† This use of saliva, commonly and superstitiously used by the Greeks and Romans to avert harm from " the evil eye," or as a fetish against anything baneful or unlucky, is very remarkable. The washing in the pool is enjoined in order to complete the cure by the expiatory or lustral virtue of water.

‡ The Sinaitic and Beza rightly read, " He went away therefore, and washed himself, and returned seeing."

12. And they said to him, Where is that man? I know not, said he.

13. They bring to the Pharisees him who was once blind;

14. And it was the Sabbath on the day when Jesus made the mud and opened his eyes.*

15. Again therefore he was asked, and (now) by the Pharisees,† *how* he had recovered his sight. And he said to them, He put mud on my eyes, and I washed myself, and I have my sight.

16. Hereupon some of the Pharisees began to say, This man is not from God, for he does not keep the Sabbath; and others said, How can a man who is a sinner do such signs? And there was a schism between them.

17. Accordingly they said to the blind man again,‡ What say *you* about him, that he

---

* The story perhaps is not authentic, but inserted to illustrate the oft-repeated charge of the Pharisees that Jesus was breaking the law of the Sabbath. The narrative occupies the whole chapter, and has much repetition.

† "Again therefore the Pharisees also asked him" (R.V.).

‡ The Sinaitic reads, "They say therefore to him who was formerly blind, Again therefore what dost thou say about thyself, that," etc. The Beza, "they said therefore to the blind."

opened your eyes? And he said, That he is a prophet.

18. The Jews therefore did not believe concerning him that he had been blind, and had recovered his sight,* until they had called the parents of the man himself who had been restored to sight, and asked them, saying,

19. Is this your son, of whom ye say that he was born blind? How is it then that he sees now?

20. Accordingly his parents answered and said, We know that this man is our son, and that he was born blind.

21. But how it is that he now sees, we know not; or who opened his eyes, *we* know not†; ask himself,‡ he is of age; he will speak about himself.

22. These words said his parents, because they were in fear of the Jews; for already the Jews had come to an agreement, that if any-

---

* This clause, "that he had been," etc., is omitted in the Beza.

† The man had told others (11), "It was the man that is called Jesus."

‡ The Sinaitic omits this clause.

one should confess him (to be) Christ,* he should be put out of the assemblies.

23. That was why his parents said, He is of age, ask himself.

24. For the second time therefore they summoned the man who had been blind, and said to him, Give glory to God ; *we* know that this man † is a sinner.

25. Upon this he replied, Whether he be a sinner, I know not ; one thing I know, that whereas I was blind, at this present time I see.

26. They said to him therefore, What did he do for you ? *how* did he open your eyes ?

27. He answered them, I have told you already, and ye heard not. Why then do ye desire to hear it again ? Can it be that ye also want to become his disciples ?

28. And they abused him,‡ and said, You *are* a disciple of that man ; but we are disciples of Moses.

29. *We* know that God hath spoken to

---

* That is, the promised and expected Messiah.
† Viz., who, as you say, cured you.
‡ Viz., for making an impudent suggestion.

Moses;* but as for this man, we know not whence he is.

30. The man answered and said to them, Why, herein is the marvel, that *ye* know not whence he is, and (how) he opened my eyes.†

31. We know that our God heareth not sinners; but if any one be a worshipper of God, and do his will, him he heareth.

32. From all time it has not been heard that anyone opened the eyes of a man born blind.

33. If this man were not from God, he could do nothing.‡

34. They answered and said to him, In sins wert thou begotten wholly; and art *thou* for teaching *us*? And they cast him out.

35. (Now) Jesus was told that they had cast him out; and having found him he said, Dost *thou* believe in the Son of man? §

---

* The Beza adds, "And that God hears not sinners" (from 31).

† Possibly πῶς has dropped out; or it may be implied from πόθεν. This was the question in 26. There seems no logical force in A. and R.V., "and (yet) he opened," etc. The man wonders that they are still ignorant, though they have been told so plainly. Perhaps καὶ τίς, "and who it was that," etc.

‡ Viz., in such a case as this.

§ That is, the Messiah. The Beza and Sin. agree in this

36. And who is he, sir, he said, that I may have faith in him?

37. Said Jesus to him, Thou hast both seen him and he who is speaking with thee *is* he.*

38. And he said, I believe it, sir; † and he made obeisance to him.

39. And Jesus said, For judgment ‡ came I into this world, that those who see not may see, and those who see may become blind.

40. (Now) those who were with him of the Pharisees heard these (words), and said to him, Are *we* also blind?

41. Said Jesus to them, If ye were blind, ye would not have sin; but as it is, ye say, We have our sight: (therefore) your sin remaineth.§

---

reading. "The Son of God" (A. and R.V.), the reading in Stephen's text, must be considered as of less authority.

* See iv. 26.

† The usual rendering, "Lord, I believe; and he worshipped him," seems stronger than is justified by the Greek. The man expresses his belief that it must have been the Messiah himself who cured him, and kneels or prostrates himself before him.

‡ Or perhaps, "for separation" or "distinction" (viz., of those who can and those who cannot see wonders wrought), in order to enlighten the humble and to confound the proud.

§ Because you can see the works done, and yet refuse to believe.

X.

1. VERILY, verily I say unto you, He that enters not through the gate into the sheep-fold, but ascends from another side, that man is a thief and a robber.

2. But he who does enter by the door is a shepherd of the sheep.*

3. To him the door-keeper opens, and the sheep hear his voice, and his own sheep he calls by name, and leads them out.

4. [And] when he has turned out all his own sheep, he goes in front of them, and his sheep follow him† because they know his voice.

5. But with a strange man they will not go, but will flee from him, because they do not recognise the voice of those strange to them.

6. This short saying Jesus spoke to them,

---

* The Beza reads, "is himself the shepherd of the sheep."
† Or, "keep up with him."

but they (on their parts) were not aware what things they were that he was talking to them about.*

7. Again therefore Jesus said, Verily, verily I say unto you, *I* am the door to the sheep.

8. All that came before me † are thieves and robbers; but ‡ the sheep did not hear them.

9. *I* am the door; if any one has entered through me, he shall be kept safe,§ and shall go in, and go out and find pasture;

10. (Whereas) the thief comes not except on purpose to steal, and slay, and destroy. *I* came that they may have life, and have (all they want) in abundance. ‖

11. I am the Good Shepherd,¶ (and) the Good Shepherd lays down his life for the sheep.

---

* Or, " did not know the meaning of what he was saying to them "

† The Sinaitic omits "before me."

‡ That is, ("And they tried to call them), but," etc.

§ Like a flock protected from the attack of the wolf. Compare 27, 29.

‖ This last clause is wanting in the Beza. The Sin. reads, "that they may have life everlasting."

¶ Or, "that good-looking shepherd," viz., represented familiarly in art, e.g., on gems and cameos.

12. (But) he who is a hireling, and is not the shepherd, whose own the sheep are not, beholds the wolf coming and leaves the sheep to themselves and flies, and (so) the wolf seizes them and scatters them.

13. Because he is a hireling and has no concern for the sheep.

14. (But) *I* am that Good Shepherd, and I know mine, and mine know me.

15. Even as the Father knows me and I know the Father; and I lay down my life for the sheep.

16. Other sheep also I have, which are not of this * fold; those also I must bring, and they will hear my voice, and they shall become one flock, one shepherd.†

17. This is why the Father loves me, ‡ because I am laying down my life that I may get it back.

18. It was not that any one took it from

---

* Viz., the Jewish.

† This reads like a later addition at a time when the Petrine and Pauline, Jewish and Gentile, schools were at variance.

‡ The too familiar English, "is so fond of me," is nearer the Greek.

me,* but that I am laying it down of myself. I have leave † to lay it down, as I also have leave to take it back. Such is the commandment I received from my Father.

19. A schism again took place among the Jews, on account of these words,

20. And many of them began to say, He is possessed, and is mad; why do ye still listen to him?

21. Others said, These sayings are not those of one that hath a demon;‡ can an evil spirit § open the eyes of the blind?

22. At that time there took place the Encænia ‖ at Jerusalem. It was winter,

23. And Jesus was walking in the temple in Solomon's porch.

24. Accordingly the Jews surrounded him and kept saying to him, How long dost thou

---

* The Beza has, "no one takes it from me."
† Or, "right" (R.V.), or power, or "full liberty."
‡ The exact sense, "one who is being demonized," or "acting the part of a demon," can hardly be expressed.
§ Neither "demon" nor "devil" represents the Jewish notion of possession by some evil influence with supernatural yet bodily power over man.
‖ "The feast of the dedication" (A.V.).

keep our soul in suspense? If thou art the Christ, tell us freely.

25. Jesus replied to them, I did tell you, and ye believed not:* the works which I do in the name of my Father, these † bear witness of me.

26. But ye have not faith because ye are not of *my* sheep. ‡

27. Those sheep that are mine hear my voice, and I know them, and they go with me,

28. And I give them life everlasting, and they shall not perish for all time, and no one shall snatch them out of my hand.

29. What my Father hath given me is greater than all; § and no one is able to snatch out of the Father's hand.

30. I and the Father are one. ‖

---

* The Beza has, "I do tell you, and ye believe me not."

† The Beza has, " of themselves bear witness."

‡ The Beza adds, "even as I told you," which perhaps belongs to the next verse.

§ The Beza reads, "My Father who has given (them) to me, is greater than all." The Sinaitic reading is intermediate between the two, having μείζων, not μείζον.

‖ That is (probably), in mind, and intention, and in absolute

31. Again (therefore) the Jews carried in their hands * stones that they might stone him.

32. Jesus replied to them, Many good works did I display to you from the Father; for what work of them (all) are ye for stoning me?

33. The Jews answered him, For a *good* work we stone thee not, but for blasphemy, and because thou, being (but) a man, makest thyself God.†

34. Jesus answered them, Is it not written in your law that 'I said, Ye are gods?'‡

35. If he called those gods to whom the word of God did come, (and the Scripture cannot be broken),

36. Do *ye* say of him whom the Father hallowed and sent into the world,§ Thou

---

agreement of *will*. The Jews seem to have taken the words in a different sense.

* "Took up stones" (A. and R.V.). "Baiulaverunt ergo lapides" (Beza) is more correct than "sustulerunt ergo lapides" (Vulgate).

† Compare v. 18. The Sinaitic omits "and" before "because." ‡ Psalm lxxxii. 6.

§ Here again Jesus clearly claims to be the Messiah.

blasphemest, (and that) because I said, I am the Son of God?

37. If I do not the works of my Father, believe me not.

38. But if I do them, even if ye put not faith in *me*, have trust in my works, that ye may be aware and make up your minds * that as the Father is in me, so I am in the Father.

39. Again (therefore) they sought to take him by force, and (again) he got away from their hands,

40. And went off a second time to the other side of the Jordan, into the place where John was at first baptizing, and there he made some stay.†

41. And many came to him, and they began to say, that John indeed wrought no sign, but all that John said about this man was true.

42. And many believed on him there.

---

* "That ye may know and understand" (R.V.). The Beza has only, "that ye may know." The Sinaitic, "that ye may know and have faith."

† The imperfect tense. The Beza has the aorist, "he took up his abode," literally, *et mansit ibi*. So also the Sinaitic.

XI.

1. NOW there was one lying ill, Lazarus of Bethany, from the village of Mary and her sister Martha.

2. And it was the (same) Mariam that anointed the Master with fragrant essence,* and wiped his feet with her hair, whose brother Lazarus was sick.

3. Accordingly, the sisters sent to him † saying, Master, lo! he whom thou lovest is lying ill.

4. And Jesus having heard it said to her, This illness is not unto death,‡ but (it was sent)

---

* We have no word to express exactly the composition of olive oil with different kinds of scent (described by Lucretius, ii., 547—53), *distillation* and *alcohol* being unknown to the ancients. Our term "Ointment" conveys a different idea.

† The Beza reads, "sent to Jesus," and "this illness of his," in 4.

‡ Dr. Westcott remarks on this, "The actual occurrence of death was in no way against this statement." It is not easy to see this. The real meaning seems to be, "This illness will

for the glory of God, that the Son of God may be glorified through it.*

5. Now Jesus was fond of † Martha and her sister, and of Lazarus (also).

6. When therefore he had heard that he was sick, at the time indeed he remained in the place where he was for two days,

7. (But) then, after this, he says to his disciples, Let us go into Judæa again.

8. Say the disciples to him, Rabbi, just now the Jews were seeking to stone thee, and (yet) thou art going back again there.‡

9. Jesus answered, Are there not twelve hours in the day? If one walks in the day, he does not stumble, because he sees the light of this world.

10. But if one walks in the night, he stumbles, because the light is not in him.§

---

not *end* in death, even if, to display the power of God, a temporary death ensues."

* The reading of the Sinaitic is made up of two ancient variations, (1) "but for the glory of God," and (2) "but that the Son of God may be glorified through it."

† The Beza has, ἐφίλει, "loved."

‡ Or, interrogatively, "and art thou going there again?"

§ "In it," the Beza, *i.e.*, in the night. The answer is obscure and ambiguous (see ix. 5). The point seems to be,

11. These are the very words that he spoke;* and after this he said to them, Lazarus, our friend, has fallen asleep;† but I am going that I may awaken him.

12. The disciples therefore said to him, Master, if he has fallen asleep he will recover.

13. But Jesus had spoken about his death, whereas *they* fancied that he was speaking about the repose of sleep.

14. Accordingly, Jesus then said to them in plainness of speech, Lazarus is dead,‡

15. And I am glad on your account, in order that ye may believe, that I was not there; but let us go to him.

16. Thomas therefore,—he who is called Didymus,—said to his fellow-disciples, Let us also go that we may die with him.§

---

that as Christ is the light of the world, that which is to be done must be done while the light is shining. Therefore he will return to Jerusalem.

* Possibly ταυταυτα is the transcriber's mistake.

† The Beza, here and in ver. 12, has the present tense, "is sleeping."

‡ Literally, "died," viz., at the time when you hoped he might be recovering. The Beza has, "Lazarus our friend."

§ That is, die with our Master, who will assuredly be in danger of death by stoning (see ver. 8).

17. Jesus therefore having arrived,* found that he had now been four days in the tomb.

18. Now Bethany was near Jerusalem, about fifteen furlongs distant.

19. And many of the Jews had come to Martha and Mariam that they might console them about their brother.

20. Martha then, when she heard that Jesus was coming, went to meet him; but Mary kept sitting in the house.

21. Martha then said to Jesus, If thou hadst been here, my brother would not have died.

22. And now I know, † that whatsoever things thou shalt ask of God, God will give thee.

23. Says Jesus to her, Your brother shall rise again.

24. Says Martha to him, I know that he will rise again at the resurrection on the last day.

25. Jesus said to her, I am the Resurrection and the Life; he that has faith in me shall live, even if he be dead;

26. And every one who is now alive and

---

* The Beza has, " came to Bethany and found," etc.
† The Beza reads, "but even now I know."

has faith in me, will not die for all time. Believest thou this?

27. She says to him, Yea, Master, I believe that thou art the Christ, the Son of God, who is coming into the world.*

---

* The Jews were so impressed with the coming of a promised Messiah that they readily—with minds predisposed for the supernatural—accepted the credentials of cures which were reported miraculous. Those who believe in "spiritism" are equally ready, even in this age of science, to accept as true manifestations, real or supposed, of supernatural agency, not less wonderful than the miracles which they reject. When once Christ, believing himself to be the Messiah, called himself by the equivalent title, "Son of God," his followers, in spite of the monotheistic feeling of the Jews, proceeded to place Son and Father side by side, and regard them as co-equals. And thus, while generally distinguishing, St. Paul occasionally so nearly identified the Sender with the Sent that (1) the apotheosis, (2) the doctrine of the two Divine Persons, and (3) the Trinity became logically inevitable.

In the Fourth Gospel, Christ is the Logos, the worker of signs of his Divine mission, the Son obedient to the call to give his life for the salvation of man. St. Paul, setting the reported miracles aside, and even the miraculous incarnation, but believing he had *personal* evidence of and *direct* call from the risen Christ, takes up the theory of atonement and propitiatory sacrifice as the central point of his teaching. There was a reason for this which can be plainly stated. The ancient sun-worshippers in the valley of the Euphrates, whose traditions found a ready response in the Semitic mind, regarded human sacrifice as a divinely-appointed form of expiation. For a parent to give his only son to be slain on the altar was the highest act of obedience and devotion

28. And having said this she went away and called her sister Mariam, having told her privately,* The Teacher is here, and is calling for you.

29. And she, when she heard it, arose quickly and went to him.

30. Now Jesus had not yet come into the village, but was still in the place where Martha had met him.

31. The Jews therefore who were with her in the house and were comforting her, having noticed that Mariam had got up quickly and gone out, followed her, supposing that she was gone to the tomb to weep there.†

(see on iii. 16); and *the voluntariness of the surrender was the measure of the merit.* This appears in many of the legends of self-immolation in classical antiquity.

It is not really easy to reconcile the totally different views, (1) that Christ was put to death by the Jews because he had offended them by his teaching; (2) that he *gave himself* up to death as a willing victim for the salvation of mankind. Between these views there is really nothing in common. Yet it is by the transition of the one into the other that the teacher, reformer, friend of sinners, the enemy of pride and formalism, in the synoptic Gospels, becomes the "Lamb of God Who is bearing the sins of the world," under the later aspects of his office and mission.

* Or, "called privately." The Beza has, "in silence."

† That is, "to pay the tribute of loud wailing and lamenta-

32. Mariam then, when she had come where Jesus was, on seeing him fell at his feet, saying to him, Master, if thou hadst been here, my brother would not have died.

33. Jesus therefore, when he saw her weeping and the Jews weeping who had gone out with her, he chafed in his spirit,* and inwardly vexed himself,

34. And said, Where have ye laid him? They say to him, Master, come and see.

---

tion for the dead." The Greeks from early times regarded this as one of the solemn duties to be paid to one deceased, the omission of which would prevent his rest. The Sinaitic reads, "thinking that Jesus was (is) going to the tomb," etc.

* The compound is used in Æsch., *Theb.*, 461, of the impatient neighing of a horse. In other passages of the New Testament it conveys the idea of chiding and dissatisfaction. Hesychius gives the sense of "issuing orders under threat." It is to be regretted that a word so important to such a narrative should be extremely uncertain. The version "groaning" has no authority. It is impossible to give a rendering that is quite satisfactory. The idea is, " he bitterly reproached (was angry with) himself," viz., for having been absent. The Vulgate has, "infremuit spiritu et turbavit seipsum." The meaning seems to be that he allowed his naturally tranquil demeanour to be roused to the expression of emotion. The Beza reads, " he was disturbed in the spirit as one angry with himself."

35. Jesus wept.*

36. The Jews therefore said, Behold how he loved him.

37. And some of them asked,† Could not this man, who opened the eyes of one that was blind, have caused that this man also should not die?

38. Jesus therefore again inwardly chafing goes to the tomb; and it was a cave with a stone lying close against it.‡

39. Says Jesus, Remove the stone. Says Martha to him,—the sister of him that had died,—Master, by this time he stinks, for he has been dead four days.§

40. Says Jesus to her, Did I not tell you

---

* The very short phrase hardly expresses the meaning according to our idiom. We should say, "burst into tears." or "shed tears at the words." Both the Beza and the Sinaitic read, "And Jesus wept."

† Gr., *said*.

‡ To close the entrance.

§ Dr. Westcott well observes, that this (the incipient putrefaction) is given not as a fact, but as expressing the fear or surmise of the sister.

The Greeks had peculiar ideas about the "third day" after death. Till that had expired, they thought the spirit was yet within call, and the apparently dead might be in a trance. (See the curious injunction of Hercules, who has restored Alcestis

that, if you will have faith, you will see the glory of God?

41. Accordingly they removed the stone, and Jesus raised his eyes upwards and said, Father, I give thee thanks that thou heardest me.

42. And *I* knew that at all times thou dost hear me; but (yet) on account of the crowd standing around I said it, that they may believe that it was thou who didst send me.

43. And having said these (words), in a loud voice he cried, Lazarus, come hither out of (the tomb).*

44. Forth came the dead man, having his feet and his hands tied with bandages,† and his face was bound round with a towel. Says

---

from the grave, not to speak to her *till the third day has come* (Eur., *Alcest.*, 1146). Special rites (τρίτα or πρότριτα) were paid to the ghost on that day.

* The literal call, *hither, outside!* is rather remarkable. The loud summons for the dead to appear, or return to life, is nearly the same in Æsch., *Pers.*, 687, καὶ ψυχαγωγοῖς ὀρθιάζοντες γόους οἰκτρῶς καλεῖσθέ μ'.

† Literally, "cuttings" of cloth. The limbs, observes Dr. Westcott, may have been swathed separately, as was the Egyptian fashion.

The difficulties in this stupendous miracle are of course great, and they are not really met by Dr. Westcott's remark, that if the fact is denied, and a conclusion is come to that the

Jesus to them, Untie him, and let him go his way.

45. Many therefore of the Jews,—those who had come to Mariam and *seen* what he had done,—believed in him.

46. But some of them went off to the Pharisees, and told them what things Jesus had done.*

47. Accordingly the chief priests and the Pharisees convened a meeting, and said, What are we to do? † For this man is working many signs.

---

scene was an imposture or the record a fiction, " both of these hypotheses involve a moral miracle."

It is not stated that the *narrator* was present; yet the narrative is very circumstantial, and it would seem from ver. 45 that there were a considerable number of spectators, evidently prepared to witness some marvellous act.

In the next chapter we read of Lazarus residing with his family, as if nothing unusual had happened to him. Then we read that the Jews wished to put Lazarus to death.

To restore a dead man to life is to inflict on him the pain of dying again. It may be a demonstration of Divine power, or a favour to surviving friends; but we are reminded of the Homeric verse (Od., xii., 22), "Unhappy wretches, who have to die twice, while other mortals die but once."

* Probably, as there seems to be emphasis on "having seen," these others went, not immediately, perhaps, to tell the wonderful tidings that a dead man had been recalled to life.

† Literally, " What are we for doing?"

48. If we let him off as we are now doing, all will believe on him, and the Romans will come and take away both our place and our nation.

49. But one of them, Caiaphas, being high-priest that year, said to them, *Ye* know nothing.

50. Nor do ye consider that it is your own interest that one man should die in behalf of the people, and the whole nation perish not.*

51. Now this he said, not of himself, but being high-priest for that year he spoke for them with a prophetic foresight† that Christ was about to be put to death in behalf of the nation.

52. And not *only* on behalf of the nation, but in order that he might also bring together into one the children of God that are scattered.

---

* Either you must punish this pretended Messiah, or he will proclaim himself King, and draw upon you the wrath of the Romans. See xviii. 14.

† Properly, προφητεύειν is not "to predict," but to speak as the mouthpiece of another. The two senses seem here combined; the Evangelist wishes to show, that the words used, "the whole nation perish not," had an ulterior meaning, viz., the uniting under one headship under a common Saviour. Hence he seems to attribute to the speech of the chief priest a greater weight than a private opinion.

53. From that day therefore they took counsel that they might put him to death.

54. Jesus therefore no longer walked with freedom* among the Jews, but departed thence into the region near the wilderness,† to a city called Ephraim, and there he stayed with the disciples.

55. Now the Passover of the Jews was nigh, and many had gone up to Jerusalem out of the country that they might purify themselves.‡

56. They sought therefore for Jesus, and spoke with one another as they stood in the temple, What do *ye* think? That he will not come to the feast?

57. Now the chief priests and the Pharisees had given commands, that if any one should be aware where he was, he should give information, that they might lay hands on him.

---

* Or, literally, "in free conversation."

† The Beza adds a word which is perhaps the corrupted name of the region (σαμφουρειν).

‡ By the sprinkling with hyssop, etc. The Beza and Sin. read, "before the Passover, that," etc.

XII.

1. JESUS therefore six days before the Passover came to Bethany, where Lazarus was,* whom Jesus had raised from the dead.

2. They made therefore† for him a dinner there, and Martha served, but Lazarus was one of those reclining (at table) with him.

3. Accordingly Mariam taking a pound of fragrant essence, (made) of nard used for sipping,‡ of great price, anointed the feet of Jesus, and wiped with her hairs his feet; and the house was filled with the scent of the essence.

---

* The Beza adds, "who had been dead."

† The Beza reads, "and they made," etc.

‡ Probably of the kind described by Pliny, N.H. xii. 12, as of "pleasant taste," and used (as Eau de Cologne now is) to drink in small sips, to give fragrance to the breath. The epithet (from πίνω) is the same as the πιστὸν φάρμακον, "a draught," in Æsch., *Prom.*, 480. It occurs also in Mark xiv. 3, where the anecdote is given with some differences. See also Matthew xxvi. 6.

4. But Judas Iscariot, one of his disciples,— he who was soon to betray him,—said (to her),

5. Why was not this essence sold for three hundred denars* and given to the poor?

6. Now this he said, not because he cared for the poor, but because he was a thief, and having the burse,† he had the carrying of whatever was thrown (as alms).

7. Jesus accordingly said, Let her be,‡ that she may keep it against the day of my entombment.

8.§ For the poor ye have always with you, but me ye have not always.

---

* Nearly as many francs.

† From Pollux, x., 153, it would seem that this was the name of the case in which flutes and their mouthpieces were carried. Either from the shape, or from the allusion to γλῶσσα, it meant also a box (or satchel) in which alms and contributions of food were collected. Judas, it seems, would have preferred the offering stored away in the burse. This anecdote suggests a curious picture of the lowly disciples and their Teacher going about to collect alms of all kinds.

‡ Literally, perhaps, "dismiss her" (from the charge, or from blame). The Revised Version has, "suffer her to keep it against the day of my burying." Only a very small portion would have been used for anointing, and the remainder could be reserved.

§ The Beza omits this verse, and continues thus: "And a great multitude of the Jews had heard that he was (is) there, and had come," etc.

9. A great multitude* then from the Jews was aware that he was there; and they came not only on account of Jesus, but that they might also see Lazarus whom he had raised from the dead.

10. But the chief priests also took counsel that they might even put Lazarus to death,

11. Because it was through him that many of the Jews went off and put their trust in Jesus.

12. On the morrow the multitude† that had come to the feast, having heard that Jesus was coming into Jerusalem,

13. Took the leaf-stems of the palm-trees and went forth for the purpose of meeting him, and cried aloud, Osanna! blessed is he that comes in the name of the Lord and (as) the King‡ of Israel.

---

* Both here and in ver. 12 the article is prefixed to the noun, ὁ ὄχλος πολύς, in the Vat. It is omitted in the "textus receptus" of 1552 and in the Beza, but only in 12 in the Sinaitic. There must have been two separate readings, ὁ ὄχλος, and ὄχλος πολύς, and the two have been unskilfully combined. The united phrase *could* not mean "the common people."

† Omitting here the word πολύς. The Beza and Sinaitic read, "a great multitude," and the latter, "having come."

‡ The Beza reads simply, "the King." The triumphal entry is recorded in all the Gospels. Christ accepts the prof-

14. And Jesus having found a young ass, sat upon it, even as it is written,

15. 'Fear not, Daughter of Zion ; behold, thy King cometh sitting on an ass's colt.'

16. These things understood not his disciples at first ; but when Jesus had been glorified,* then remembered they that these (words) had been written about him and these (things) they had done to him.

17. The multitude therefore that was with him when he called Lazarus forth from the tomb and raised him from the dead, bare witness.

18. It was for this also that the multitude had gone to meet him, because they had heard that he had done this sign.

19. The Pharisees therefore said to themselves, Ye see that ye are doing nothing that

---

fered honours of the multitude (the lower classes, doubtless) *as the Messiah.* To be hailed publicly as "king" was an exceedingly dangerous position. It was this event, it may be said, that sealed his fate. The title was treasonable in the Roman view, and the scoffing title set over the cross by Pilate's order marked *his* disapproval of the claim.

* That is, perhaps, when he had attained his full renown and reputation. See on ii. 11, and below 24.

avails aught; lo! the world* is gone off after him.

20. Now there were certain Greeks† of the number of those who were going up that they might worship at the feast.

21. These accordingly came to Philip from Bethsaida of Galilee, and asked him saying, Sir, we desire to see this Jesus.

22. Philip goes and tells Andrew; (accordingly) Andrew comes with Philip,‡ and they tell Jesus.

23. And Jesus answers them saying, The hour is come for the Son of Man to be glorified.§

24. Verily, verily I say unto you, Unless the grain of the corn should fall on the ground and

---

* The Beza has, "the whole world."

† "Apparently proselytes of the Gate."—*Dr. Westcott.*

‡ Literally, "comes Andrew and Philip and they say," etc. The Sinaitic reads, "and again comes Andrew and Philip;" the Beza, "again" (without *and*) "Andrew and Philip tell Jesus."

§ The precise meaning of this verb, of such frequent occurrence in the New Testament, is not clear; but our '(military) word "glory" does not convey the same idea as the Greek term, which is rather that of bringing to men's thoughts, or into the highest repute. The "Doxology" seems to turn on this attribution of δόξα, the conclusion of the mind as to the ineffable greatness of God.

die, it remains only itself;* but if it dies, it bears much fruit.

25. (Even so) he who loves his life causes it to perish,† and he who cares not for ‡ his life in this world will keep it for life everlasting.

26. If any one ministers to *me*, let him follow *me*, and where I am, there also this server§ of mine will be; if any one ministers to *me*, the Father will honour him.

27. Now is my soul troubled; and what should I say? Father, bring me safe out of this hour? Yet it was for this that I came into this hour.

28. Father, glorify my name? ‖ There came

---

* Without productiveness.
† The Beza reads, "will lose it."
‡ Literally, "hates it," as if anxious only to be rid of it. The followers of Christ even to death, and the spread of his teaching by those means, seem referred to.
§ The emphasis is marked as Dr. Westcott suggests. Both the verb and the noun are rendered by "serve" and "servant" (A.V. and R.V.).
‖ Usually rendered without interrogation, and with the reading of the Sinaitic, Beza, and Vulgate (probably the true one) "thy name." The Beza reads, "glorify thy name in (or with) the glory which I had with thee before the world was created," *i.e.*, as the Logos. Here it may be remarked that supernatural voices, as in Mark i. 11, Acts ix. 4, form a com-

accordingly a voice out of the sky, 'I have both glorified it, and I will glorify it again.'

29. (Then) the crowd who stood and heard it, said there had been thunder. Others said, An angel hath spoken to him.

30. Jesus answered and said, It is not for * *me* that this voice has come, but for *you*.

31. Now is the judgment of this world; † now is the ruler of this world about to be cast out.

32. And I, if I be raised on high from the earth,‡ will draw all men§ to myself.

33. Now this he said, signifying by what kind of death he was about to die.

---

mon feature in the portents of classical antiquity (Eur., *Bacch.*, 1078; *Iph. T.*, i., 1385; *Androm.*, 1147), and not much weight can be given to evidence of alleged events in which deception is so extremely easy.

* Literally, "through," "on account of."

† Not meaning, "Now the world will be brought to trial for sin," but, "Now it will decide whether it will be for me or against me."

‡ On the cross, like the healing serpent in the wilderness (see iii. 14). A word is used suitable also to the Ascension. But the obvious meaning is, that as the Israelites were drawn or attracted to the brazen symbol in the hope of a cure, so mankind shall be drawn to their Healer and Saviour on the cross.

The Beza and Sin. read, "all things."

34. The crowd therefore answered him, *We* heard out of the law that the Christ remains for all time; and how is it that *you* say that the Son of Man must be raised up? Who *is* this Son of Man?

35. Jesus therefore said to them, Yet for a little time the light is among you; walk while ye have the light, that darkness may not overtake you; and he who walks in the dark knows not where he is going.

36. While ye have the light, believe in the light, that ye may become sons of light. These (words) spake Jesus, and went off and was hidden from them.

37. But though he had done so many signs in their presence, (yet) they believed not on him.

38. That the saying of Esaias the prophet might be fulfilled, which he spake, ' Lord, who had trust in that which we heard, and to whom was the Lord's arm displayed?'

39. (And) it was for this cause that they were not able to believe,—for that again Esaias had said,

40. 'He has blinded their eyes and he hardened their hearts, that they might not see

with their eyes and perceive with their heart and be turned, and I should heal them.'

41. Thus said Esaias, because* he saw his glory,† and spoke about *him*.

42. Nevertheless, even of the rulers many believed on him, though on account of the Pharisees they did not confess (him), that they might not be excluded from the assembly.

43. For they were fond rather of their reputation with men, above (their zeal for) the glory of God.‡

44. And Jesus cried aloud and said, He that has faith in me has not faith in *me*, but in him who sent me;

45. And he that beholds *me* beholds him who sent me.

46. I have come a light into the world, that he who has faith in me may not remain in the dark;

---

* The Beza reads, "when he saw the glory of his God."
† Dr. Westcott observes: "St. John identifies the Divine Person seen by Isaiah with Christ" (as the Logos). He also remarks that the latter quotation (Isa. vi. 10) "differs alike from the Hebrew and the LXX." The former citation is Isa. liii. 1. The Beza here reads, "he has blinded thine heart, that," etc.
‡ The Beza reads, "rather than the glory," etc.

47. And if any one hear my sayings and keep them not,* *I* judge him not; for I came not to judge the world, but to save the world.

48. He that rejects me and receives not my sayings has (already) one that judges him : the word which I spoke, that it is that will judge him in the last day.

49. For I spoke not of myself, but the Father who sent me has himself given me a command as to what I should say and what I should speak about.

50. And I know that his commandment is everlasting life. The (words) therefore that *I* speak, even as the Father has told (them) to me, so do I speak.

---

* The Beza omits " not."

XIII.

1. NOW before the feast of the Passover Jesus, knowing his hour had come that he should pass out of this world to the Father, after having fondly loved his own who were in the world, (showed that) his love for them was complete.

2. And as dinner was going on,* the accuser having now put it into his heart that Judas, son of Simon, (called) Iscariot, should betray him;

3. (Jesus) knowing that the Father had committed all things into his hands, and that as he had come forth from God, so (now) he was going to God,

4. Rises from the dinner and lays down his outer garments, and taking a towel girded himself (therewith).

---

* The Beza reads, "was over."

5. Next he put water into the wash-pot, and began to wash the feet of his disciples, and to wipe them with the towel wherewith he was girt.

6. Accordingly he comes to Simon Peter; (but he) says to him, Master, washest thou my feet?

7. Jesus answered and said to him, What I am doing, you understand not now, but you will know afterwards.

8. Says Peter to him, Never for all time shall thou wash *my* feet! Jesus answered him, If I wash thee not, thou hast no part with me.

9. Says Simon Peter to him, (Then), Master, (wash) not my feet only, but my hands also and my head.

10. Says Jesus to him, He that has been (cleansed) in the bath has no need to do more than to wash his feet,* but he is clean all over; clean too are ye, but not all.

11. (For he knew him that was betraying him; therefore said he, Not all of you are clean).†

---

* The Beza reads, "has no need to wash his head, but only his feet, for he is clean," etc.

† The Beza omits the latter half of this verse.

12. When therefore he had washed their feet and taken up his outer garments and again reclined (at table), he said to them, Are ye aware what I have done for you?

13. You call me (by the names) The Teacher, and The Master; and ye say well, for (such) I am.

14. If then *I* washed your feet, your Master and your Teacher, (so) ye also* are bound to wash each other's feet; †

15. For I gave you an example, that even as I did to you, so ye also should do (to each other).

16. Verily, verily I say unto you, The slave is not greater than his master,‡ nor the envoy greater than he who sent him.

17. If ye know these things,§ blessed ye are if ye do them.

---

* The Beza reads, "how much more are you also bound," etc.

† That is, to show similar tokens of love and humility or self-denial. It is curious that the *literal* foot-washing has passed into a Church-rite.

‡ Or, "owner."

§ "The lessons conveyed by the feet-washing."—*Dr. Westcott.*

18. It is not about all of you that I speak ; *I* know what persons I chose for myself ; but (it has so happened) that the Scripture may be fulfilled, ' He that eats my bread raised against me his heel.'*

19. I tell you now at once, before it has come to pass, that ye may believe, when it has come to pass, that I Am.†

20. Verily, verily I say unto you, He that receives any one I may have sent,‡ receives me ; and he that receives me receives him who sent me.

21. When Jesus had spoken thus he was troubled in his spirit, and bare witness§ and said, Verily, verily I say unto you, that one of *you* is about to betray me.

22. The disciples looked at each other,|| doubting of whom he was speaking.

23. (Now) there was one of his disciples

---

* Psalm xli. 9.

† See on viii. 58.

‡ It is likely that ἄν τινα was originally ὅντινα (*quemcunque misero*, Beza). The Apostles are meant.

§ Viz., that one of the Twelve was a traitor to him.

|| The Sinaitic gives, "The Jews therefore looked at each other, the disciples," etc. This is a vestige of an ancient double reading.

leaning back on the bosom of Jesus,—that one who was the favourite of Jesus.*

24. To him therefore Simon Peter nods, and says to him,† Say who he is of whom he speaks.

25. He (then), having fallen back after this fashion‡ on the breast of Jesus, says to him, Master, who is it?

26. Jesus therefore replied, It is he for whom I shall dip the sippet, and give it to him. Accordingly he dipped a sippet, and took and gave it to Judas (the son) of Simon Iscariot.

27. And after the sippet, § then entered Satan into him. Jesus therefore says to him, What thou art for doing, get done quickly.

---

* The custom of reclining at meals on a divan (*torus*) was precisely the same with Jews, Greeks, and Romans; it was the ancient and general custom of the East.

In this case, "St. Peter, sitting (reclining) in the second place (of honour) was not in a favourable position for hearing any whisper, which would fall naturally on the ears of St. John" (in the third place).—*Dr. Westcott.*

† The Beza reads, " to find by inquiry who this might be of whom he spoke (speaks)." So also the Sinaitic.

‡ The Beza and Sinaitic omit, "after this fashion." ("He leaning back, as he was," R.V.)

§ The Beza omits this clause. The reading is made up of two, (1) "then," and (2) "after the sippet."

(28. Of this none of those reclining were aware, *why* he said it to him ;

29. For some thought, as Judas had the burse, that Jesus said this to him, Buy what we have need of for the feast ; or that he might give something to the poor.)

30. He therefore after he had taken the sippet went out immediately ; and it was night.

31. When therefore he had gone out, Jesus says, Now is the Son of Man glorified,* and God is glorified in him ;

32. And God will glorify him in himself, and will glorify him forthwith.†

33. Little children, yet a little while I am with you. Ye shall seek me, and even as I said to the Jews, that where I go, ye cannot come, so I say to you now.

34. A new commandment do I give you, that ye love one another,—that even as I loved you, so ye also may continue to love each other.‡

---

* Or brought to honour and repute. See on ii. 11.

† Christ seems to say that his death and reunion with the Father are close at hand.

‡ This passage seems made up from two ancient readings,

35. By this shall all men know that ye are my disciples, if ye have love one to the other.

36. Says Simon Peter to him, Master, where are you going to? Jesus answered, Where I go, you cannot now follow me, but you shall follow me later on.

37. Says Peter to him, Master, *why* am I not able to follow thee even now? I will lay down my life for thee.

38. Jesus answers, Thy life thou wilt lay down for me? Verily, verily I say unto thee, the cock shall not crow till thou hast denied me thrice.

---

(1) " that ye may love each other even as I loved you ; " and
(2) " that even as I loved you, ye also may love each other." The same particle (ἵνα expresses " that " in both clauses.

XIV.

1. LET not your heart be troubled; you put your trust in God; put your trust also in me.*

2. In the house of my Father there are many dwelling-places. If it were not so, I would have told you that I am going to prepare a place for you; and if I do go and

3. Prepare you a place, I am coming again, and (then) I will take you to myself,† in order that where I am, ye also may be.

4. And as to *where* I am going, ye (already) know the way.‡

5. Says Thomas to him, Master, we do *not* know where thou art going; how (then) do we know the way?

---

* Or, "trust in God and in me;" or, "as ye trust in God, so trust in me."

† "To *my own* house," as it were.

‡ "Ye know, and the way ye know" (Beza).

6. Jesus says to him, *I* am the way, and the truth, and the life: no one comes to the Father except through me.

7. If ye had known me, ye would have known * also my Father; even now ye know him and have seen him.†

8. Philip says to him, Master, show us ‡ the Father, and we are content.

9. Jesus says to him, Have I been so long a time with you, and do you not know me, Philip? He that has seen me *has* seen the Father. How is it that *you* say, *Shew* us the Father?

10. Will you not believe that I am in the Father and the Father is in me? These words which (I speak) § to you I speak not from myself (the Father speaks them); and the Father abiding in me does *his* works.‖

---

* The Sinaitic has, "ye will know, and even now ye will know him." The Beza, "Ye will know, and even now ye know him."

† That is, *in me*.

‡ That is, "point him out to us."

§ The Sinaitic reads, ἃ ἐγὼ λαλῶ ὑμῖν. The older reading probably was ἃ λέγω ὑμῖν, whence Vat. ἃ ἐγὼ ὑμῖν.

‖ Though *apparently* mine, both words and works are *his*.

11. Believe *me* (when I tell you) that I am in the Father and the Father in me; or if not, believe me on account of his works.*

12. Verily, verily I say to you, he who believes in me shall himself also do the works that I do; yea, he shall do greater works than these, because I am going to the Father,

13. And whatever ye may ask in my name, that I will do, that the Father may be glorified in the Son.

14.† If ye shall have asked me anything in my name, that I will do.‡

15. If ye love me, ye will keep § these my commandments.

16. And I will ask the Father, and he will give you another advocate, that there may be with you for ever that spirit of truth which the

---

* Cod. Sin., εἰ δὲ μή, τὰ ἔργα αὐτὰ πιστεύετε. Cod. Vat., διὰ τὰ ἔργα αὐτοῦ π. Cod. Bezœ, διὰ τὰ ἔργα αὐτὰ πιστεύετε.

† Ver. 14, if the text is right, must have been a variant reading, or an independent statement of the promise just above. But *perhaps* not τοῦτο ποιήσω, but τοῦτο ποιήσετε was the old reading in ver. 13 (*i.e.*, you shall work any miracles in my name).

‡ Originally, perhaps, τοῦτο δώσω.

§ The Beza has, "keep."

world cannot receive because it beholds it not nor knows it.*

17. Ye know it because it abides with you and *is* † in you.

18. I will not let you go ‡ as orphans; I am coming to you.

19. Yet a little while and the world beholds me no longer; but *ye* behold me,§ because I live and ye shall live.‖

20. In that day ye will know that I am in my Father, and ye in me, and I in you.¶

21. He that has (received) my commandments and keeps them, he it is who loves me, and he who loves me will be loved by my Father, and I will love him and manifest myself to him.

22. Says Judas to him,—not the (one called) Iscariot,—Master, what has come to pass that you are about to manifest yourself to *us*, and not to the world?

---

* For "it" the Beza (not the Sin.) gives, "him."
† "Will be in you," the Sinaitic.
‡ Or, "*dismiss* you" (as my companions).
§ We should expect θεωρήσετε. The "Second Coming" seems referred to.
‖ "But ye behold me: because I live, ye shall live also" (R.V.). The meaning may be, "Ye will be alive when I return."
¶ Or, "and that as I am in you, so ye are in me."

23. Jesus answered and said to him, If any one loves me, he will keep my word, and my Father will love him, and we will come* to him, and make our stay with him.

24. He who loves me not keeps not my words, and the word which ye hear is not mine, but the Father's who sent me.

25. These things I have spoken to you while abiding with you;

26. But the Advocate, the Holy Spirit,† which the Father will send in my name, he shall teach you all things, and remind you of all that I said to you.‡

27. *I* give up peace for you; § *my* peace I

---

* The Beza has, "I will come and make," etc.

† The Sinaitic has, "will send the Holy Spirit," adding (by mistake of ὁ for ὅ), "the Father in my name."

‡ The Beza has, "may have said to you."

§ That is, a *worldly* peace you are not likely to have. The Vat. (not the Sin.) has ἐγὼ before εἰρήνην, which lays emphasis on the person.

The proper meaning of ἀφίημι is, I relinquish, resign, give up, cast away, etc. ("*I leave*" is from the Vulg. *relinquo*, and gives a wrong sense, "I bequeath"). The Beza version has, "pacem dismitto vobis." The sense may possibly be, "I am letting go (from heaven)," *i.e.*, I will dispatch to you Peace, as one is said ἀφεῖναι, to let a bird fly out of the hand. So Milton in the "Ode to the Nativity," "But he, her fears to cease, Sent down the meek-eyed Peace," etc.

give you ; not as the world gives it do *I* give it to you ; (therefore) let not your heart be troubled nor cowardly.

28. Ye heard that I *said*, I am going away and returning to you. If ye loved me, ye would have rejoiced at my going to the Father, for the Father is greater than I.

29. And now I have told you before it happens, that when it has happened ye may believe.

30. I will not now speak more at length with you ; * for the ruler of the world is coming, and it is not that he has anything in me,†

31. But that the world may know that I love the Father, and even as the Father gave me a command, so I do. Arise, let us go hence.

---

* Quite literally, "I shall not any more say many things with you."

† Cod. Bezæ has, καὶ ἐν ἐμοὶ οὐκ ἔχει οὐδὲν εὑρεῖν, "et in me non habet nihil invenire." Vulgate, "et in me non habet quicquam." However translated, the meaning is obscure. The sense may be, "I am about to come under the power of the Romans, and though no crime will be found in me, I shall suffer in testimony of my love," etc. See xii. 31.

XV.

1. I AM the real vine, and my Father is the husbandman.

2. (If there be) any branch on me that does not bear fruit, he removes it, and every such as does bear fruit he prunes* in order that it may produce yet more.

3. Already *ye* have been pruned and dressed † through the word which I have spoken to you.

4. Abide in me as I (abide) in you.   Even

---

* Literally, " clears," " dresses," viz., from superfluous leaves and side-shoots. The Beza reads, " will clear."

† Lit., " ye are clean," like well-pruned trees.

‡ This is certainly the true meaning of an idiomatic expression. See v. 17, and compare Æsch., *Eum.*, 140, ἔγειρ᾽, ἔγειρε καὶ οὐ τήνδ᾽, ἐγὼ δὲ σέ; Eur., *Bacch.*, 364, πειρῶ δ᾽ ἀνορθοῦν σῶμ᾽ ἐμὸν, κἀγὼ τὸ σὸν. " Do you support me, as I support you." For " abide in " the Greek is " remain on." But though the branch is on the stem, the stem is not " on " the branch. The Beza omits ver. 3, and the first half of ver. 4.

as the branch cannot bear fruit of itself, unless it remain on the vine, so neither (can) ye, unless ye abide in me.

5. I am the vine, ye are the branches; he that abides in me, and I in him, he it is that bears much fruit; (I say this) because apart from me ye can do nothing.

6. If any one abides not in me, he is cast out * as the vine-branch (from the vineyard) and withers away; and (then it is that) they gather them up † and throw them into the fire, and they are burnt.

7. If ye abide [not] ‡ in me, and my sayings abide in you, ask whatsoever ye will, and it shall be done to you.

8. Herein is my Father glorified, that ye may bear much fruit, and become *my* disciples.

9. Even as the Father loved *me*, (so) I also

---

* As the vine-clippings are carried off from the vineyards. Tacit., Ann., xi., 32, "vehiculo quo purgamenta hortorum excipiuntur."

† Viz., the clippings or dressings when they are withered and dry. The Beza reads, "and they gather it up;" Lat., *et congregant illud*. So also the Sin.

‡ The negative is wrongly added.

loved *you*. Abide * in this love of mine (for you).†

10. (And) if ye shall have kept my commandments, ye *will* abide in my love, even as I have kept the Father's commandments, and abide in *his* love.

11. These (words) have I spoken unto you that this *my* joy may be in you, and *your* joy may be made full.‡

12. This is *my* commandment, that ye love one another, even as I loved you.

13. Greater love than this not any one has,—that one should lay down his life in behalf of his friends.

14. *Ye are* my friends, if ye continue to do § what I command you.

---

* That is, perhaps, "continue to show to others the same love which the Father has shown to me, and which I have shown to you." The reading of the Sinaitic is here remarkable: "Abide in this love of mine even as I also kept the commandments of my Father and abide in his love," μου being wrongly repeated after τὰς ἐντολάς.

† "The love that answers to my nature and my work."—*Dr. Westcott.*

‡ That we may both rejoice in the confidence of mutual love.

§ The Beza reads, "for ye are—if ye shall have done."

15. I no longer call you servants,* because the servant knows not what his master is doing; but *you* I have called friends, because all things that I heard from my Father I made known to you.

16. It is not that you chose out me for yourselves, but that I chose you, and put you in this position, that ye might go hence and bring forth fruit, and that your fruit may be lasting, that whatsoever ye ask the Father in my name, he may give it to you.

17. Such are my commands to you,† that ye love one another.

18. If the world hates *you*, ye are well aware that it has shown its hatred to *me* before it did to you.‡

19. If ye were of the world, the world would show love to its own; but as ye are not of the

---

* Or rather, "slaves."

† Dr. Westcott takes this verse as "the introduction of a new line of thought, and not as the summing up in conclusion of what has gone before." It is true, the antithesis to *love*, viz., *hate*, is now added; but it seems directly suggested by the foregoing.

‡ Literally, "it has hated me first in respect of you."

world,* but I chose you for myself out of the world, therefore does the world hate you.

20. Bear in mind the saying which I told to you, that the servant is not greater than his master. If they persecuted me, they will persecute you too; if they kept my word, they will also keep yours.

21. But all these things will they do to you for my name's sake, because they know not him that sent me.†

22. If I had not come and spoken to them, they would not have had ‡ sin; but as it is they have no excuse concerning their sin.

23. He that hates me, hates my Father also.

24. If I had not done among them the works which no one else (ever) did, they would not have had sin; but as it is, they have even seen

---

* Instead of this clause the Beza reads, " because ye were of the world."

† That is, *but* the opposition and the hatred will arise from ignorance of a Divine mission.

‡ The remarkable form εἴχοσαν represents the Latin *habuissent* and the older Greek οὐκ ἂν ἔσχον. The Beza reads, οὐχ εἶχαν.

(them) and (yet) they have hated both me and my Father.*

25. But it is to the end that the word may be fulfilled that is written in their Law,† that they hated me without a cause.

26. When the Advocate has come, whom I will send to you from the Father, (even) the Spirit of truth that goes forth from the Father,‡ *he* will bear witness about me.

27. But ye likewise do (now) bear witness of me, because § ye have been with me from the beginning.

---

* " But now have they both seen and hated both me and my Father " (A.V. and R.V).

† Psalm xxxv. 19.

‡ The author of the treatise entitled " Philopatris," attributed to Lucian, must have read this passage, § 12, where he speaks satirically of the doctrine of the Trinity, υἱὸν πατρὸς, πνεῦμα ἐκ πατρὸς ἐκπορευόμενον, ἐν ἐκ τριῶν καὶ ἐξ ἑνὸς τρία.

§ Or, " that ye have been with me (been my disciples) from the first."

XVI.

1. THESE (words) have I spoken to you that ye may not* be made to trip;†

2. (For) they will cause you to be shut out from their assemblies, (and not only that,) but the hour is coming when any one who may have put you to death will think he is offering a service to God.

3. And all this they will do because they have no knowledge of the Father nor of me.

4. But these (words) have I spoken to you, that when the time for them‡ has come, ye may remember them, that *I* said them to you.

---

* The Sin. omits "not."

† Or, "scandalised," "offended" (A.V.), "be made to stumble" (R.V.) The opposition to the disciples' teaching seems to be meant, such as might cause a check and a discouragement.

‡ Literally, "the hour of them."

But I said them not to you at the first, because I was with you.*

5. And now I am going to him who sent me, and (yet) not one of you asks me, Where art thou going?

6. But because I have uttered these (words) to you, this grief has filled your heart.

7. But *I* tell you the truth; it is expedient for you that I should depart; for if I do not depart, the Advocate will not come to you; but if I should go, I shall send him to you,

8. And he, when he comes, will bring a charge against the world about sin, and about righteousness, and about judgment.

9. About sin, because they have not† faith in me;

10. And about righteousness, because I am going to the Father, and you behold me no more;

11. And about judgment, because the ruler‡ of this world has been judged.§

---

* "The departure of Christ is the condition of the coming of the Paraclete."—*Dr. Westcott*.

† The Sin. omits the "not."

‡ "He will show that the world is wanting in the knowledge of what sin, righteousness, and judgment really are."—*Dr. Westcott*.

§ These three verses form an extremely obscure passage,

12. I have yet much to say to you, but ye cannot bear it now.

13. But when he has come,—the spirit of truth,—he will guide you into all truth. For he will not speak from himself, but what he hears he will speak,* and of the things that are coming he will bring you the tidings.

14. He it is that will glorify *me*, because he will take of that which is mine, and bring it as a message to you.†

15.‡ All things that the Father has are mine;§ for this cause said I that he takes of what is mine and will bring it as a message to you.

---

of which it is difficult to find any satisfactory explanation. Possibly the meaning of the last is, "Because the wickedness of the Roman world has been denounced." See xiv. 30.

* Literally, "as many things as." This passage is remarkable as constructively teaching a Trinity of Persons. "The fact which is declared is, that the teaching of the Spirit comes finally from the one source of truth. The words that follow show that no distinction is made in this respect between that which is of the Father and that which is of Christ."—*Dr. Westcott.*

† It is not easy to render ἀναγγελεῖ. "He will show" (A.V.); "he shall declare" (R.V.)

‡ The Sinaitic omits ver. 15.

§ The expression seems to reflect the familiar proverb, κοινὰ τὰ τῶν φίλων, "friends possess all things in common."

16. A little while and ye no longer behold me, and again a little while and ye shall see me.

17. (Some) of his disciples therefore said to each other, What is this that he says to us, A little while and ye behold me not, and again a little time and ye shall see me; and that* I go to the Father?

18. Therefore they kept on saying,† What *is* this that he says, A little while? We know not.

19. Jesus was aware that they desired to ask him,‡ and said to them, Is it about this that ye question among yourselves, because I said, A little while and ye behold me not, and again a little while and ye shall see me?§

---

* Or (in reference to ver. 10), "and because I go." (Thus A.V. and R.V.) The Sin. gives ω (probably for ὥς).

† The Beza omits this clause.

‡ The Sin. reads, "intended to ask him."

§ If words have any meaning, and are not framed to deceive, Christ here promised his early return; and this, it is well known, was the fixed belief of the Church in the first age. When the fourth Gospel was written, disappointment at the non-appearance had begun to set in. But the modern attempts to explain away these and similar declarations are futile. The followers of Jesus were taught to look for his return from heaven, and they built all their hopes upon it.

20. Verily, verily I say unto you, that *ye* will weep and wail, but the world will rejoice;* *ye* will be grieved, but your grief will be turned into joy.

21. The wife,† when she is in travail, has sorrow because her hour is come; but when she has given birth to the child, she thinks no more of the anguish through the joy (she feels) at the birth of a human being‡ into the world.

22. So ye also now indeed have grief, but I shall see you again,§ and your heart will rejoice, and your joy no one shall take from you.

23. And on that day ye shall ask *me* nothing; verily, verily I say unto you, if ye shall have asked anything of the Father, he will give it you in my name.

---

* As being freed from a reformer who condemned its ways. —*Dr. Westcott.*

† Literally, "the woman (of the family)."

‡ "A man" is not the true rendering of ἄνθρωπος, which not unfrequently means "a woman;" indeed, the term sounds harsh when applied to a newly-born infant. The Sin. adds the article, "the man," or, "one who is a man" (human).

§ See the note on ver. 19.

24. Till now ye asked nothing in my name; ask* and ye shall receive, that your joy may be made full.

25. These things have I spoken to you in short sayings. The hour is coming when I shall speak to you no longer in short sayings, but in plain words shall report to you† of the Father.

26. In that day ye shall ask‡ in my name: and I do not tell you that *I* shall ask the Father about you,

27. For the Father himself loves you because ye have loved me and have believed that I came forth from the Father.

28. I came out from the Father and I have come into the world; again I leave the world and go to the Father.§

---

* "The command [in the present imperative] implies continuous prayer, and not [as the aorist would] a single petition."—*Dr. Westcott.*

† As if in a message brought from heaven on the return to earth. The constant account of himself that Christ gives, as one *sent*, introduces a phraseology based on the idea of returning, reporting, sending other envoys, coming back again, etc., etc.

‡ The Sin. reads, "ask."

§ The writer appears to contemplate Christ as the incarnate Logos, who will return to God from whom he proceeded.

29. His disciples say, Lo! *now* thou dost speak in plain words, and utterest no short saying ;

30. *Now* we know that thou knowest all things, and hast no need that any one should ask thee. Herein is our belief that thou camest from God.

31. Jesus answered them, Do ye now believe ?* Behold, the hour cometh and is come for you to be dispersed, every one to his own, and leave me alone. And (yet) I am not alone, because the Father is with me.

33. These (words) have I spoken to you, that in me ye may have peace. In the world ye have † tribulation, but take courage ; *I* have overcome the world.

---

* Or, "Ye believe *now*" (though before ye were not fully convinced). Or, perhaps, "*Do* ye now at last (ἄρτι) believe ?"

† The Beza reads, "ye will have."

XVII.

1. THESE things spake Jesus, and lifting up his eyes to the heaven he said,* Father, the hour is come; glorify thy Son that the Son may glorify thee,

2. As thou didst give him power over all flesh, that all which thou hast given to him he may give to them,† (even) life eternal.

3. And this is the eternal life, that they know thee the only true‡ God, and him whom thou didst send, (even) Jesus Christ.

4. I glorified thee on the earth by finishing the work which thou hast given me to do,

5. And now do thou glorify me, Father, with

---

* Dr. Westcott remarks that the prayer seems to have been spoken aloud, and that "such words, however little understood at the time, were likely to be treasured up, and to grow luminous by the Divine teaching of later experience."

† The Sin. reads, "I may give to him;" the Beza, "that everything thou hast given to him may have," etc.

‡ Real or genuine, as opposed to false gods.

thyself, with the glory which I had with thee before the world was.

6. I made manifest thy name to the men whom thou gavest me out of the world. Thine they were, and to me thou gavest them, and thy word they have kept.

7. Now they know* that all things which† thou gavest me are from thee,

8. Because the words which thou gavest me I have given to them, and they received them themselves, and concluded truly that I came forth from thee, and they believed that it was thou who didst send me.

9. It is about them that I make my request; it is not about the world that I make it, but about those whom thou hast given me, for that they are thine,

10. And all things that are mine are thine, and thine mine,‡ and I have been glorified in them.

---

* They have arrived at the opinion or conviction. The Sinaitic has, "now I know," etc., and omits below the verb translated "concluded," as does also the Beza MS.

† Literally, "as many as."

‡ The familiar saying, κοινὰ τὰ τῶν φίλων, is again had in view. But the Sinaitic reads, "and to me thou gavest them;" the Beza, "and thou didst glorify me in them."

11. And I am no longer in the world, whereas they are themselves in the world, and I am departing to thee. Holy Father, keep them in thy name in which thou hast given (them) to me, that they may be one even as we also (are one).

12. When we were * with them, I kept them in thy name in which thou hast given (them) to me, and I guarded them and not one out of them was lost, except the son of the doom, that the Scripture may be fulfilled.

13. But now I return to thee, and these things I speak in the world that they may have this joy of mine in full measure in themselves.

14. I have given them thy word, and the world hated † them, because they are not of the world, even as I am not of the world.

15. My request is not that thou mayest remove them from that which is evil ; ‡

---

* Codd. Sin. and Bez., ὅτε ἤμην, "when I was," etc. The Beza reads, "Whom Thou hast given me I kept." The Sin. omits "in which," etc.

† Or, "hates," or, "has hated." Beza gives the present tense.

‡ The Sinaitic has, "from out of the world," and adds, "but that thou mayest keep them from that which is evil ;" and so the Beza MS. Clearly the Vat. reading is wrong. The R.V. translates, "I pray not that thou shouldest take

16. They are not of the world, (even) as I am not of the world.

17. Consecrate them* to truth; this word of thine *is* the truth.

18. As thou didst send me into the world, so I also sent them into the world,

19. And in their behalf I devote myself, that they also may be devoted in (the cause of) truth.

20. And not respecting these only make I my request, but also respecting those who through their word believe on me,

21. That they may all be one; even as thou, Father,† (art) in me, and I in thee, that (so) they may themselves also be (one) ‡ in us, that the world may believe that it was thou who didst send me.

22. And the glory which thou hast given to me I have given to them, that they may be one, even as we (are) one,

---

them from the world, but that thou shouldest keep them from the evil *one*" (note, "Or, *evil*").

* Lit., "Make them holy in (the) truth."

† The nominative seems here and in Beza miswritten for the vocative, as in vers. 24, 25.

‡ The word "one" is added in the Sinaitic, but is wanting in Vat. and Beza.

23. I in them and thou in me, that they may be brought into a perfect unity, that the world may know that it was thou who didst send me, and didst love them * even as thou lovedst me.

24. Father, as to what thou hast given me, I desire that where I am, they also may be with me, that they may behold this glory of mine which thou gavest me, for that thou didst love me before the foundation of the world.

25. O righteous Father, as ‡ the world knew thee not, though I knew thee, and these knew that it was thou who didst send me,

26. So I made known to them thy name, and will make it known, that the love wherewith thou lovedst me may be in them as § I (am) in them.

---

* The Beza reads, "and I loved them."

† A promise of fulfilling one of three or more wishes is more than once alluded to in ancient literature.

‡ This seems the meaning, in our idiom, of "*both* the world knew thee not—*and* I made known," etc. See on xv. 4.

§ Literally, "and I in them."

XVIII.

1. HAVING spoken these words Jesus went out with his disciples to the other side of the torrent of the Cedars,* where was a garden, into which he himself entered and his disciples.

2. And Judas also, who was betraying him, knew the spot, because on many occasions Jesus had resorted with his disciples to that place.

3. Judas therefore having received the company of soldiers and (others) under his orders † from the chief priests and the Pharisees, arrives there with lights and torches and a heavy-armed force.

4. Jesus therefore, knowing all that was com-

---

* "The brook Cedron" (A.V.) "The brook Kidron (R.V.) separated the Mount of Olives from the Temple-mount."—*Dr. Westcott.* The Beza and Sinaitic read, "the torrent of Cedrus."

† "Officers" (A.V. and R.V.)

ing upon him, went forth and said to them, Whom seek ye?

5. They answered him, Jesus the Nazarean. Jesus said to them, I am (he). There stood there also with them Judas who was betraying him.

6. When therefore he said to them, I am (he), they went backward and fell to the ground.

7. Again therefore he asked them, Whom seek ye? And they said, Jesus the Nazarean.

8. Jesus answered, I told you that *I* am he. If therefore ye seek *me*, let these go their way.

9. (This he said) that the word might be fulfilled which he had spoken,* that "Whom thou hast given me, of them I lost not one."

10. Thereupon Simon Peter having a sword,† drew it, and struck the high priest's servant, and cut off his right ear;‡ and the servant's name was Malchus.

11. Jesus therefore said to Peter, Put that

---

* Viz., xvii. 12.

† Or long knife in a sheath. The Beza reads, "Then Simon Peter," etc. "Simon Peter therefore" (R.V.)

‡ Or, perhaps, "lobe of the ear," *auriculam*.

sword into the sheath; the cup which the Father hath given me, shall I not drink it?

12. Accordingly the band of soldiers and the chiliarch,* and those of the Jews who were under orders, arrested Jesus and put him in bonds,

13. And took him to Annas first, for he was father-in-law of Caiaphas, who was high priest that year.†

14. (Now this Caiaphas was he who had advised the Jews that it was to their interest that one man should die in behalf of the people.)

15. Now Simon Peter was accompanying Jesus, and another disciple; and that disciple was known to the high priest, and had gone in with Jesus into the court of the high priest.

16. But Peter had taken his stand at the door outside. Accordingly this other disciple—he that was an acquaintance of the high priest—went out and spoke to the woman who was keeping the door, and brought in Peter.

17. This maid therefore, who kept the door, says to Peter, Surely *you* are one of the disciples of this man. Says he, I am not.

---

* Commander of a cohort.
† From this verse to xx. 15 is wanting in the Beza.

18. Now the servants and those under orders had made a charcoal fire, and were standing there, for it was cold, and they were warming themselves ; and Peter also was with them standing and warming himself.

19. The high priest therefore questioned Jesus about his disciples and about his teaching.*

20. Jesus answered him, *I* have spoken in plain words to the world ; *I* on all occasions taught in assembly † and in the temple, where all the Jews are wont to meet, and in secret I spoke nothing.

21. Why askest thou me ? Ask those who have heard what I spoke to them : see,‡ *these* know what *I* said.

22. And when he had said this, one of those under orders who was standing by gave Jesus a slap, saying, Is that the way you answer the chief priest ?

---

* " This preliminary examination was directed to the obtaining (if possible) of materials for the formal accusation which was to follow."—*Dr. Westcott.*

† That is, where there was a crowd of followers collected to hear me. " In synagogues " (or synagogue) R.V. " In the synagogue," A.V.

‡ Or perhaps, " See (to it, for) these," etc.

23. Jesus answered him, If I spoke badly, give evidence of what was bad; but if well, why smitest thou me?

24. (Now) therefore Annas sent him bound to Caiaphas the high priest.

25. Now Simon Peter was (still) standing and warming himself. They said therefore to him, Surely *you* also were of the number of his disciples. He denied it, and said, I am not.

26. Says one of the servants of the high priest, being a relation of him whose ear Peter had cut off, Did not *I* see you in the garden with him?

27. A second time then Peter denied it, and immediately a cock crew.

28. Accordingly they conduct Jesus from Caiaphas into the court-house; and it was (yet) early, and they themselves did not enter the court-house that they might not be defiled,* but might eat the Passover.

29. Pilate therefore went out to them and said, What charge do ye bring against this man?

---

* " By entering a house from which all leaven had not been scrupulously removed."—*Dr. Westcott.*

30. They answered and said to him, If this man were not a doer of evil, we should not have given him up to thee.

31. Pilate therefore said to them, Do *ye* take him, and judge him according to *your* law. Said the Jews to him, *We* are not allowed to put any man* to death.

32. (This took place) that the saying of Jesus might be fulfilled, which he spoke † signifying by what kind of death he should die.

33. Pilate therefore again entered into the court-house and called Jesus, and said to him, Is it *you* who are the King of the Jews? ‡

34. Jesus answered, Do you say this of yourself, or did others tell you about me?

35. Pilate answered, Surely *I* am not a Jew; it was your nation and the chief priests § that gave you up to me. What was it that you did?

36. Jesus answered, This kingdom of mine is not of this world. If *my* kingdom were of

---

* The copy from which the Sinaitic was transcribed would seem to have had "any Jew," or, "any one of the Jews."
† Viz., xii. 32.
‡ That is, the person calling himself so.
§ The Sinaitic has, "and the chief priest."

this world, those who are under service to me *
would strive that I should not be given up to
the Jews. But as it is, *my* kingdom is not from
hence.

37. Thereupon Pilate said to him, Then are
you a king? † Jesus answered, It is *you* who
say that I am a king.‡ It was for this that I have
been born, and for this that I have come into
the world, that I may bear witness to the truth.
Every one who is of the truth § hears my voice.

38. Says Pilate to him, What *is* truth? ∥
And having said this he went out again to the
Jews, and said to them, *I* find no crime in him.

---

* The Sinaitic adds "also," *i.e.*, as well as those under
your command ("my servants," R.V.; in note, Or, "officers").

† That is, a king at all, or in any sense, if not of the Jews or
of this world.

‡ Dr. Westcott rightly gives the meaning of the reply, viz.,
that Christ "neither definitely accepts nor rejects the title."
It seems a formula meaning, "it may be so; you said so; I
did not." It is remarkable that in all the Gospels the same
emphatic use of the pronoun occurs in the answer to this question. The common rendering seems to imply acquiescence in
the charge, "thou sayest it." The note here in R.V. is
altogether untenable, "Thou sayest it, because I am a king."

§ "Who draws from the truth the inspiration of his life."—
Dr. Westcott.

∥ Not in the abstract, but in any particular case, as in the
weighing of evidence.

39. But there is a custom of yours, that I should set free one (prisoner) at the Passover. Do ye therefore desire that I should release to you this king of the Jews?

40. Again therefore they raised an outcry, saying, Not *him*, but Barabbas! Now this Barabbas was a bandit.

XIX.

1. ACCORDINGLY Pilate then took Jesus and scourged him.

2. And the soldiers having twined a crown of thorns, put it on his head, and threw round him a mantle of purple.

3. And they kept coming up to him and saying, Hail, thou King of the Jews! and giving him slaps.*

4. And Pilate went out again,† and said to them, See, I am bringing him out to you that ye may be made aware that I find no legal charge against him.‡

5. Accordingly Jesus came forth wearing the

---

* The imperfect tenses. The soldiers, of course, thought to show their loyalty by mocking at what they supposed were rival claims to be a king of Judæa.

† "Pilate had returned within the prætorium to order the scourging."—*Dr. Westcott.*

‡ Or, "no crime in him" (A.V.).

thorny crown and the purple robe, and (Pilate) said to them, See, this is a man.*

6. When therefore the high priests and those under their orders saw him, they raised a yell, saying, Crucify him, crucify him! Says Pilate to them, Take him and crucify him yourselves, for *I* find not in him any guilt.

7. The Jews answered him, *We* have a law, and by that law he is bound to die, because he made himself the Son of God.

8. When therefore Pilate heard this speech he was more afraid,†

9. And he entered into the court-house‡ again, and said to Jesus, From what place do *you* come? But Jesus gave him not a reply.

10. Pilate therefore says to him, Speak you

---

* "Behold, the man" does not seem a correct rendering. Pilate wished (as Dr. Westcott remarks) to excite some feeling of compassion at the sight; here was a human being, a fellow-creature (ἄνθρωπος, xi. 50), not a mere scape-goat, that was being made a victim. But the Sinaitic reads "the man." This would mean, "the man whom I said I was going to bring out to you."

† Viz., lest the outcry against Jesus should lead to a riot, or (12), lest he should be accused at Rome.

‡ The *prætorium*, or head-quarters of the officer exercising military jurisdiction.

not (in answer) to *me* ? Know you not that as I have authority to release you, so I have authority to crucify you ?

11. Jesus answered him, Thou wouldst have* no authority against me if it had not been given thee from above; for this reason he that gave me up to thee† hath greater sin.

12. From this (reply) Pilate sought to release him; but the Jews raised an outcry, saying, If thou release this man thou art no friend of Cæsar's: every one who makes himself a king speaks against (the claim of) Cæsar.

13. Pilate therefore having heard these words brought Jesus outside, and took his seat on a raised platform at the place called (in Greek) Pavement, but in Hebrew Gabbatha.

14. Now it was the Preparation for the Passover, (and the time) was about the sixth hour. And he saith unto the Jews, Behold, your king.

15. Accordingly *they* (also) raised a cry, Away, away with him! crucify him! Says Pilate to

---

* οὐκ ἂν εἶχες is probably the true reading. The Sinaitic gives οὐκ ἔχεις (εχισ).

† "The high-priest, representing the theocracy."—*Dr. Westcott.*

them, Shall I crucify your king? The high priests answered, We *have* no king, unless it be Cæsar.

16. Upon this he gave him up to them to be crucified.

17. Accordingly they received Jesus from him,* and he, carrying for himself the cross, went out to the spot called, The Place of a Skull, which in Hebrew is named Golgoth,

18. Where they crucified him, and with him other two, on this side and on that, and Jesus in the middle.

19. And Pilate wrote also a title† and set it on the cross; and the writing was, Jesus the Nazarean, the King of the Jews.

20. This title therefore was read by many of the Jews, because the place of the city where Jesus was crucified was near, and it was written in Hebrew, Latin, and Greek.‡

21. The chief priests of the Jews therefore

---

* The Sinaitic reads, "And they having taken Jesus, led him off."

† That is, a label or heading setting forth the circumstances. We have no precise word to express a technical Roman term.

‡ So that any one of these nations would understand why the crucifixion had been carried out.

said to Pilate, Write not,* The King of the Jews, but that that man said, I am King of the Jews.

22. Pilate answered, What I have written I have written.

23. The soldiers therefore, when they had crucified Jesus, took his outer garments and made of them four parts, for each soldier a part, and also the (woollen) frock.† Now this frock was without seam, made by the hand-loom from the top through its whole length.

24. Accordingly they said to each other, Let us not tear it, but draw lots for it, whose it shall be. (And this took place) that the scripture might be fulfilled,‡ 'They shared my outer garments among themselves, and upon my clothing they laid a ballot.'§ These things then the soldiers did.

---

* Lit., "Do not *go on writing*, as you propose. The transcriber of the Sinaitic has omitted ver. 20 and the first half of 21, through the recurrence of "King of the Jews."

† This last clause is omitted in the Sinaitic. "Garments" and "coat" (R.V.) are very poor renderings, and "tunic" is too purely Roman. The flannel (or worsted-made) shirt of the modern waterman is very nearly the $\chi\iota\tau\acute{\omega}\nu$, except that the latter reached down to the knees.

‡ Psalm xxii. 18.

§ "Upon my vesture did they cast lots" (R.V.).

25. Now there had taken their stand by the cross of Jesus his mother and his mother's sister, Mary, the wife of Clopas, and Mary of Magdala.

26. Jesus therefore, seeing his mother,* and that disciple standing by whom he loved,† said to his mother, (Good) woman, see, (here is) your son.

27. Then he said to the disciple, See, (here is) your mother.‡ And from that hour the disciple took her to his own (home).

28. After this, Jesus, knowing that all had now been finished, in order that the scripture might be made complete,§ says, I thirst.

---

* This clause is omitted in the Sinaitic. Below, this MS. reads, "and says to his mother." This indicates some variation in very early copies,—an interesting fact, if we consider the importance and the celebrity of the text.

† Perhaps "specially loved," or, "who was his favourite disciple." The primary meaning of ἀγαπᾶν is "to hug," a demonstrative act of strong affection. It occurs frequently in this Gospel, and Jesus is ἠγαπημένος παῖς in Clement to the Corinthians 59, as Demosthenes has παῖς ἀγαπητὸς, "Mid." § 165. The verb is so used in Hom., Od., xxiii., 214.

‡ "St. John was nearest to the Virgin by ties of blood (the son of her sister)."—*Dr. Westcott.*

§ Perhaps Psalm lxix. 21. But the reference seems a forced one. We might, perhaps, translate, more nearly in our idiom, "that nothing might be wanting to the scripture."

29. (Now) there was set there a vessel full of sour wine. Having therefore put a sponge full of the sour wine on a (stalk of) hyssop,* they applied it to his mouth.

30. When Jesus therefore had received the sour wine he said, It is finished, and inclining his head he gave up his spirit.

31. The Jews therefore, as it was the Preparation, that the bodies should not remain on the cross on the Sabbath,—for that day, (the day) of the Sabbath, was a great one,—asked Pilate that their legs might be broken, and that they might be taken away.

32. Accordingly the soldiers came, and broke the legs of the first and of the other who was crucified with him.

33. But on coming to Jesus, when they saw that he was already dead,† they broke not his legs.

34. But one of the soldiers with a spear

---

* Supposed to be the caper-plant, which, says Dr. Westcott, has stems three or four feet long. The "hyssop" rather than the "reed" of the other Gospels seems introduced with the design of connecting Jesus with the Paschal Lamb.

† The Sinaitic reads, "they found him already dead and," etc.

pierced his side, and there issued forth immediately blood and water.*

35. And he that saw it has borne witness, and his witness is true.† And *he* knows that he speaks the truth, that ye also may believe.

36. For these things took place that the scripture might be fulfilled, 'A bone of his shall not be broken';

37. And again another scripture says, 'They shall look on him whom they pierced.'

38. Now after these (events) Pilate was asked by Joseph of Arimathea, who was a disciple of Jesus, (but in secret, through his fear of the Jews,) that he might carry off the body of

---

* There is great physical difficulty in the narrative. Dr. Westcott's note will hardly be regarded as satisfactory. "The issuing of the blood and water from his side must therefore be regarded as a sign of life in death (?). It showed both his true humanity and (in some mysterious sense) the permanence of his human life." The simple and obvious truth is, that the ancient belief in the expiatory effects of "water and blood" led the writer to assert that he can personally attest this (to him) convincing proof that Jesus gave up his life *in atonement and expiation for sin.*

† Literally, "genuine," not suborned, nor in any way falsified.

Jesus; and Pilate allowed him. He came therefore and carried off his body.*

39. And there came also Nicodemus,—he who had made his first visit to him at night,—bringing a packet † of myrrh and aloes, about a hundred pounds weight.‡

40. Accordingly they took the body of Jesus and swathed it in linen bands with the aromatics, as it is the custom of the Jews to entomb.

41. Now there was in the place where he was crucified a garden, and in the garden a new tomb, in which no one as yet had been laid.

42. There then, because of the Jews' Preparation,§ as the tomb was near at hand, they laid Jesus.‖

---

* The Sinaitic reads, "they came therefore and carried off," etc.

† Probably in a roll, as tobacco is now packed. There is another reading, rendered "mixture" in the versions ($μίγμα$).

‡ "The intention of Nicodemus was, without doubt, to cover the body completely with the mass of aromatics: for this purpose the quantity was not excessive as a costly gift of devotion."—*Dr. Westcott.*

§ Which prevented further attention being paid at the time to any other funeral ceremony.

‖ The Sinaitic reads, "where they laid Jesus," indicating some ancient variation.

XX.

1. NOW on the first day of the week Mary of Magdala* comes early, while it was yet dark, to the tomb, and sees that the stone has been removed from the tomb.†

2. Accordingly she runs and comes to Simon Peter and to that other disciple whom Jesus loved, and says to them, They have taken away the Master out of the tomb, and we know not where they have laid him.

3. Peter therefore went out and the other disciple, and they went on their way to the tomb.‡

4. And the two ran together, and the other

---

* The Sinaitic writes, " Mariam."
† The Sin. adds, " away from the door."
‡ The Sinaitic omits the latter clause.

disciple outran Peter, and came first to the tomb,

5. And stooping to look in,* sees the linen cloths lying; he did not however go in.

6. Simon Peter therefore comes also, closely following him, and went into the tomb; and (there) he noticed the linen cloths lying,

7. And the napkin that had been on his head not lying with the linen cloths, but by itself, rolled up (and laid) in one place.†

8. Then therefore the other disciple also went in,—he who had first reached the tomb; and he saw and believed.

9. For as yet they knew not ‡ the scripture, that he must rise again from the dead.§

---

* The technical (classical) use of παρακύψαι is to lean, head and shoulders, out of a door or window, in a stooping posture. In the above sense it occurs also Luke xxiv. 12, and below ver. 11.

† The similarity in the details of the grave-clothes and the mention of σουδάριον, both here and in the resurrection of Lazarus (xi. 44), are remarkable. The writer of the Sinaitic, whose eye had caught "the linen cloths lying," at the end of ver. 6, omits all from the same words in 5.

‡ The Sinaitic has, "he knew not."

§ "The reference is probably to Psalm xvi. 10."—*Dr. Westcott.*

10. The disciples therefore went back again to their own homes.

11. But Mary kept standing outside at the tomb weeping;* while therefore she was weeping she looked† into the tomb,

12. And beheld two angels in white (garments) sitting one at the head and one at the feet, where the body of Jesus had been lying.

13. And they say to her, (Good) woman, why weepest thou?‡ And she says to them, Because they have taken away my Master, and I know not where they have laid him.

14. Having said this she turned backwards, and saw Jesus standing, and knew not that it was Jesus.

15. Says Jesus to her, (Good) woman, why weepest thou? Whom dost thou seek? She, thinking that it was the gardener, says to him,

---

* The Sinaitic reads, "But Mariam stood in the tomb, etc."

† See on ver. 5; "she stooped and looked into" (R.V.). The Sinaitic reads, in the next verse, "and beholds angels sitting in white (garments)."

‡ The Beza reads, "whom dost thou seek?" (from 15).

Sir, if *you* conveyed him (away)* tell me where you laid him, and I will remove him.

16. Jesus says to her, Mariam. She turning says to him in Hebrew, Rabbuni, that is to say, Teacher.†

17. Says Jesus to her, Try not to touch me,‡ for I have not yet ascended to the Father; but go to my brethren and say to them, I am ascending to my Father and your Father, and my God and your God.

18. Mariam of Magdala (accordingly) goes bringing tidings to the disciples that she had seen§ the Master, and he had said these things to her.‖

19. When therefore it was late on that day,

---

* The Sinaitic reads, "if *you* are he that conveyed (carried) him away."

† The Beza has "Master" as well as "Teacher."

‡ The meaning of the *present* imperative, μή ἅπτου. This form "implies that she was already clinging to him when he spoke" (*Dr. Westcott*). But, of course, this assumes that it was not an apparition, but the bodily presence. The R.V. suggests in the note, "Or, Take not hold on me." But this would require the aorist.

§ Gk., "that I have seen." But the Beza reads, "she has seen."

‖ The Beza reads, "and what he had said to her she made known to them."

(which was) the first day of the week, and the doors being shut where the disciples were (assembled) through their fear of the Jews, Jesus came and stood in the midst,* and said to them, Peace (be) unto you.

20. And having said this he showed both his hands and his side to them. The disciples therefore rejoiced on seeing Jesus.

21. Jesus therefore said to them again, Peace (be) unto you: even as the Father hath sent me, (so) I also send you.

22. And having said this he breathed on

---

* Dr. Westcott remarks that it is vain to speculate *how* Christ came; "all that is set before us is, that he was not bound by the present conditions of material existence which we observe." But this view is absolutely contradictory to the *tangible* body represented in ver. 27, unless we assume that the risen Christ was material on one visit and immaterial at another (see on ver. 17).

It is not to be overlooked that it was a very old belief that the *wraith*, or apparition of a living person, could enter a room *with the door closed*. Thus in the Odyssey (iv., 802) the spectral form of the wife of one Eumelus holds a conversation with Penelope, having entered her bed-chamber by (as we should call it) the key-hole of the closed door.

Frequent mention is made in the Greek poets of a wraith, εἴδωλον, appearing in the likeness of a real person, *e.g.*, Od., iv., 796; Pind., ii., 36; Eur., *Hel.*, 33, 582. The account in the *Helena* is the more remarkable, because it adds the ascent to heaven of "the spiritual (air-created) body" (*Hel.*, 606).

them,* and says to them, Receive the holy spirit ;

23. If ye remit any one's sins, they *are* remitted to them ;† if ye retain any one's they *are* retained.‡

24. But Thomas, one of the twelve, he who was called Didymus, was not with them when Jesus came.

25. The other disciples therefore said to him, We have seen the Master. But he said to them, Unless I shall have seen on his hands the print of the nails, and put my finger into the print of the nails, and put my hand into his side,§ I will not believe.

---

* Literally, "blew on them." "Insuflavit in eos," Beza.

† The Sinaitic reads, "it shall be remitted (or, remission shall be made) to them." The Beza has ἀφέωνται ; the Vat. ἀφείονται. The readings of all the three, here and in Luke vii. 47, are doubtful.

‡ On this (compared with Matt. xvi. 19) Dr. Westcott remarks, "The promise, as being made, not to one, but to the society, carries with it of necessity the character of perpetuity; the society never dies." It is to be remarked that the words *might* be intended to convey the gift of healing, since in the Jewish belief there was the closest connexion between sin and bodily maladies, not so much by a physiological as by a moral law.

§ It seems clear that two ancient readings, each containing "print of the nails," and "put my hand (or finger)," have

26. And after eight days again his disciples were within, and Thomas with them. Jesus comes, the doors being shut, and stood in the midst, and said, Peace (be) unto you.*

27. Then said he to Thomas, Reach hither thy finger, and see my hands; and reach (hither) thy hand and put it into my side, and be not any longer† without faith, but have faith.

28. Thomas answered and said to him, My Master and my God.‡

29. Says Jesus to him, Because thou hast seen me thou hast believed; blessed are they that have not seen § and (yet) have believed.

---

been combined in the narrative as we have it in the Vat. The variants in the other two MSS. are very notable. The Sinaitic reads, "and have put my finger into his hand (for which there appears to have been a variant "into his side"), and put my hand." etc. The Beza, "and put my hands into his side, and put my finger into the print of the nails."

* It is remarkable that all the details of the second appearance are repeated from the first (19)

† The present imperative, $μὴ\ γίγνου\ (γεινου)$. $μὴ\ ἴσθι$ B.

‡ The reading of the Beza here may be rendered, "My Master (is) also my God," the article before $θσ$ ($Θεός$) being omitted. Christ "never speaks of himself directly as God, but the aim of his revelation was to lead men to see God in him." —*Dr. Westcott.*

§ The Sin. reads, "not seen me."

30. Many other signs then did Jesus do in presence of the disciples, which are not written in this book ;

31. But these have been written that ye may believe that Jesus is the Christ the Son of God,* and that believing ye may have life in his name.

---

* That is, the Messiah, including, perhaps, the Logos. But this is very far short of the proposition, "that Jesus is God." The Beza gives, " that Jesus Christ is the Son of God."

XXI.

1. AFTER these (events) Jesus manifested himself again to his disciples at the Sea of Tiberias; and he manifested himself in this wise.

2. There were together Simon Peter and Thomas, who is called Didymus, and Nathanael from Cana of Galilee, and the sons of Zebedee, and two others of his disciples.

3. Simon Peter says to them, I am going off to fish. They say to him, We also are coming with you. They went out and got into the boat, and that night they took nothing.

4. But when it was now early morning, Jesus stood on the beach. But the disciples knew not that it was Jesus.

5. Jesus therefore said to them, Children, have ye any meat?* They answered him, No.

---

* Or "relish to your bread." Perhaps "flesh meat, the terms σφάγιον and πρόσφαγμα being commonly applied to

6. And he said to them, Cast the net into the parts to the right of the boat, and you will (there) find (fish). They cast it accordingly, and had not strength left to draw it from* the multitude of the fishes.

7. That disciple therefore whom Jesus loved says to Peter, It is the Master. Simon Peter then having heard that it was the Master girded on his over-coat, for he was in his vest,† and threw himself into the sea.‡

8. But the other disciples came in their small boat, for they were not far from the land, but about two hundred cubits off, dragging the netful of the fishes.

9. As soon then as they had got out on to the land, they see a charcoal-fire and a bit of fish § laid over it, and a loaf.

---

victims killed at a sacrifice. Neither προσφαγεῖν nor φάγιον anywhere occur, nor are they probable forms in themselves. But Hesychius has, ὄψα· προσφάγια.

* Literally, "away from" ("for" A. and R.V.)

† The translation, "for he was naked," is doubtful. The word is applied, as in Hesiod, "Opp.," 391, to one who is wearing only the woollen frock, or inner garment; "in his shirt-sleeves," or "in his Jersey," we say.

‡ The Beza gives, "leapt," or "sprang," into the sea.

§ A diminutive is used as in vi. 9; but this so often occurs in

10. Jesus says to them, Bring of the fishes that you have caught now.

11. Simon Peter accordingly went on board and drew the net to the land quite full of large-sized fishes, (in number) a hundred and fifty-three; and for all there were so many the net was not rent.

12. Jesus says to them, Come to your morning meal. Not one of the disciples durst ask him,* Who art thou? knowing that it was the Master.

13. (Then) comes Jesus and takes the loaf, and gives it to them,† and the fish likewise.

14. This was now the third appearance of Jesus to his disciples after he had risen from the dead.

15. When therefore they had breakfasted, Jesus says to Simon Peter, Simon, son of

---

the fourth Gospel as almost to constitute one of its peculiarities. It is the same word in the next verse; the precise sense is, "morsels to be eaten with dry bread."

* Or, "put to him the searching question." The Beza and Sin. have, "but not one," etc.

† The Beza adds, "after giving thanks," but omits "and." It is remarkable that *bread and fish* seem here regarded as a sacramental meal, like the feeding of the multitude in chap. vi., and the lesson founded upon it.

John, art thou fond of me more than these? He says to him, Yea, Master. *Thou* knowest that I love thee. He says to him, Feed my lambs.*

16. He says to him again for the second time, Simon, son of John, art thou fond of me? He says to him, Yea, Master. *Thou* knowest that I love thee. He says to him, Be a shepherd to my sheep.†

17. He says to him the third time, Simon, son of John, lovest thou me? Peter was grieved because he had said to him the third time, Lovest thou me? and he says, Master, *Thou* knowest all things, *thou* art well aware that I love thee. Jesus says to him, Feed my sheep.

18. Verily, verily I say to you, when you were younger you used to gird yourself ‡ and walk about where you chose; but when you have grown old you will stretch out your hands,

---

* The Beza gives, "Feed my sheep."

† Here and below the Vat. has the diminutive, and above (15) "lambkins," with the Sin., as if to express endearment. Here the Lat. Vulg. has "feed my lambs" (not "sheep").

‡ That is, fasten or "tuck up" with a belt your long dress; *succinctus*, the Romans said.

and another * will gird you and carry you where you do not wish (to go).

19. Now this he said, signifying by what kind of death he shall glorify God.† And after he had spoken thus, he says to him, Come with me.

20. Peter turning towards him sees the disciple whom Jesus loved coming with them,— that same one who had reclined at the dinner on his breast, and had asked, Master, who is it that is betraying thee?

21. Him therefore when Peter saw, he says to Jesus, Master, and what is *he* (to do)?

22. Jesus says to him, If I will that he stay here while I am coming, what is it to thee? Come *you* with me.

23. This saying therefore went forth to the brethren, that this disciple is not to die.‡ But,

---

* The Beza gives, "and others will gird you, and take (are for taking) you away where," etc. The Sinaitic, "and others will gird you and do for you all that you do not wish."

† This seems a forced interpretation, given after the event, of words which quite naturally express senile helplessness.

‡ The Beza adds, "and they thought that that disciple," etc., and below, "that thou art not to die." The version, "I will that he tarry till I come," seems less correct,

Jesus said not to him, that he is not to die; but, If I will that he stay here while I am coming, what is it to thee?

24. This is the disciple who both bears witness about these (events), and has written these (words), and we know* that his evidence is true.

25. And there are many other things also which Jesus did, but if they shall be written one by one, I think that the world itself will not contain the books written (about them).†

though the Lat. Vulg. has, "sic cum volo manere donec veniam" (where *sic* is a provincial pronunciation of *si*, as *michi* for *mihi*). The Beza version has, "si cum volo sic manere usque dum venio"; and the Greek text has μένειν οὕτως.

* The two concluding verses form an attestation, probably from elders or brethren at Ephesus, that the narrative of this Gospel may be relied upon as true. The last clause, where the verb is in the singular, is a curious instance of extreme exaggeration. There seems to be a reference to xx. 30.

† Lit., "that are being written" ("that should be written," A. and R.V.)

www.ingramcontent.com/pod-product-compliance
Lightning Source LLC
Chambersburg PA
CBHW020251170426
43202CB00008B/324